OTHER BOOKS BY THE AUTHOR

Sacred Wells: A Study in the History, Meaning, and Mythology of Holy Wells & Waters

Water from the Sacred Well

Menhirs, Dolmen and Circles of Stone: The Folklore and Magic of Sacred Stone

The Mythic Forest, the Green Man and the Spirit of Nature

The Dark Wind: Witches and the Concept of Evil

Creatures in the Mist: Little People, Wild Men and Spirit Beings Around the World

Mysteries of Native American Myth and Religion

Ghosts, Spirits & the Afterlife in Native American Folklore and Religion

The Owens Valley Paiute

THE SWORD AND DAGGER IN MYTH & LEGEND

By Gary R. Varner
Member of the American Folklore Society

Copyright © 2007 by Gary R. Varner
Second edition © 2011 by Gary R. Varner

All rights reserved. No part of this publication may be reproduced, stored in a retrieval system or transmitted in any form or by any means without the written permission of the copyright holder.

Isbn: 978-1-257-76629-1

An OakChylde Book
Published by Lulu Press, Inc.
Raleigh, NC

Visit the author's website at
www.authorsden.com/garyrvarner

Contents

Acknowledgements	9
Introduction	11
Chapter One: A Brief History of the Sword	13
Chapter Two: The Sacred & Mythic Sword	59
Chapter Three: Sword Lore	96
Chapter Four: The Sword Dance	107
Chapter Five: The Modern Reproduction	113
About The Author	122
Bibliography	123
Index	127

Acknowledgements

I would like to thank Dr. Luigi Garlaschelli at the Department of Organic Chemistry, University of Pavia, Italy for his kind assistance in providing the photos of St. Galgano's "sword in the stone" as well as a draft copy of an article he published in Skeptical Inquirer concerning this legendary weapon.

All photographs are by the author unless otherwise noted. The illustrations not otherwise credited are public domain or the creator has surrendered any copyright ownership and has permitted them to enter public domain.

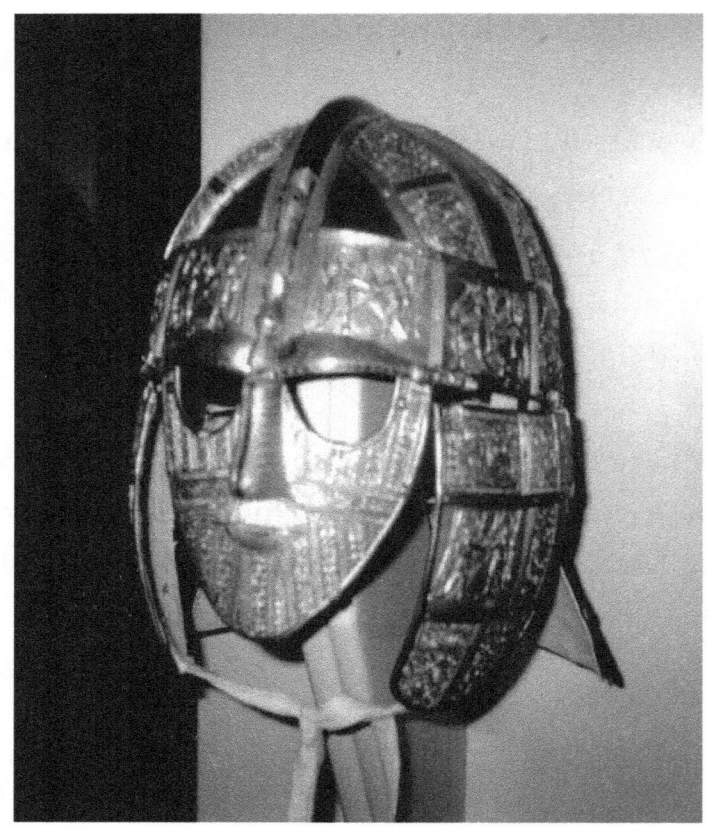

Viking helmet from Sutton Hoo. British Museum.
(Photo by Gary R. Varner)

Introduction

The sword has long been linked with mankind's stories and legends from Beowulf, Jason and the Argonauts, and King Arthur. It has also been intimately linked to stories of conquest, murder, and the destruction of ancient religions and traditions.

Perhaps not surprisingly, the sword has come to represent the male power. The sword is also symbolic of angels and other winged deities of Egyptian and Semitic cultures as well as the Islamic, Jewish and Christian religions. The sword is also used as an important symbol in Hinduism, as the flaming sword of knowledge wielded by Vishnu.

Writer Jack Tresidder wrote, "the sword is an important symbol of authority, justice, intellect and light." [1] The sword is also associated with supernatural and magic powers.

Over time the sword came to represent the person as Paul Lacroix Jacob, Curator of the Imperial Library of the Arsenal, Paris wrote, "the sword was a distinctive mark which was inseparable from the person of gentile birth."

The focus of this work will be the sword, and other bladed weapons, as they pertain to myth and legend, as well as its history, use, symbolism and supernatural power.

---

[1] Tresidder, Jack. *Symbols and Their Meanings*. New York: Barnes & Noble Books 2006, 130.

Chapter One
A Brief History of the Sword

It is not the purpose of this book to present the total history of the sword with all of its variations, types and uses but to present a truly brief overview of the bladed weapon as it evolved through time, focusing on some of the more important examples in history.

The sword has existed in its present form since the Bronze Age, before that time weapons were constructed from stone, bone and copper—all somewhat fragile in nature. Paleolithic stone weapons were very effective though. Long flint, chalcedony and obsidian blades have existed for close to a half-million years but true blades made for weapons did not occur until the Stone Age was coming to an end. "...metal knives," wrote Harold Peterson, "were already known before really good stone one became common. There is even some speculation that the development of metal knives may have spurred the design of stone weapons." [2]

Stone weapons were certainly no less deadly. In 1964 archaeologist found remains of more than 50 people, men and women, at Jebel Sahaba on the Egyptian Sudanese border. The

---

[2] Peterson, Harold L. *Daggers and Fighting Knives of the Western World.* Minneola: Dover Publications, Inc. 2001, 1.

remains clearly indicated that they had been killed with stone-bladed weapons between 12,000 and 5,000 BCE. [3]

Native American spear or knife blade, Woodland Culture, Illinois. Approx. 5" in length. (Author's collection)

Bone was also utilized as a cutting/stabbing implement in many early technologies. Bone knives were crafted into the late 19th century by American Indians and were used alongside metal weapons effectively. The photo below shows a bone-bladed weapon of the Plains Indian.

---

[3] Wills, Chuck. *Weaponry: An Illustrated History*. New York: Hylas Publishing 2006, 16.

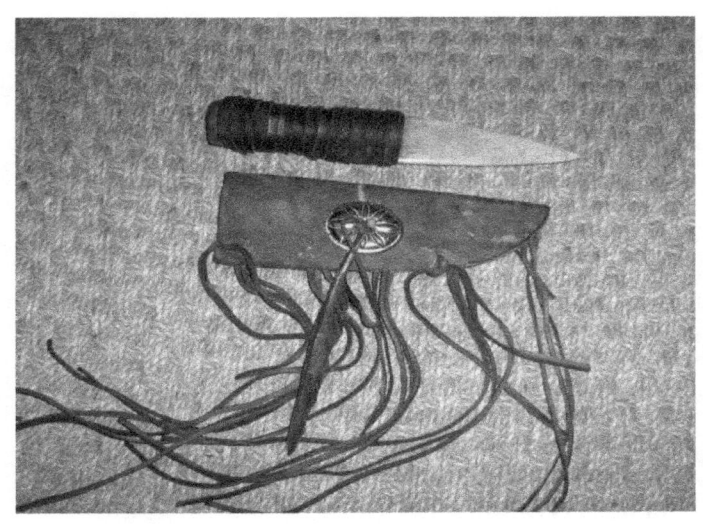

Navajo reproduction of a 19th century Sioux bone knife
(Author's collection)

True long bladed stone "daggers" originated around 1600 BCE in Scandinavia. However, very fine, decorated stone blades were crafted in Egypt around 3500 BCE [4] with handles made of bone, wood, horn or ivory. Due to the fragility of these long bladed knives, they are thought to have been more ceremonial than practical. The Scandinavian blades were created of thicker and broader stone materials, which made them very strong. The blades were made mostly of flint. The flint material used, however, came in a variety of colors, from yellow to black, green, red, and white.

---

[4] "BCE" means "Before the Common Era." "CE" means "Common Era."

Copper blades came into use in Egypt and Mesopotamia around 6500 BCE and spread into India and North America by 5500 BCE. While durable, copper is a soft metal and any usable weapon had to be made thick or wide, which significantly added to the weight of the item. Cast copper swords were manufactured up to 30-36 inches in length with a central rib added to the blade to increase the swords rigidity.

The early Minoans created weapons from copper, gold, and silver and they are also known to have developed bronze implements. With the development of bronze, around 3000 BCE in Mesopotamia, the first true swords evolved from the dagger around 2000 BCE. While the bronze sword was certainly stronger than earlier materials, it was primarily used as a stabbing weapon.

During this time the "People of the Sea," a migratory people that may have come from southern Russia arrived in the Greek islands and developed a double-edged sword with a strong point—a major development in sword design.

The use of copper and bronze has been credited with the growth of urban civilization through trade and the development of metalworking. The large tin deposits in Cornwall in western England resulted in expansive trade routes from the Mediterranean area to the British Isles. Tin is a key component in the manufacture of bronze. However this resulted in additional conflict as tin was scarcely available, mostly found in Central Europe and Britain.

It may be that the scarcity of these tin resources resulted in the next milestone of technological advancement—iron. Over time as the metal smiths figured out how to melt iron deposits using charcoal fueled furnaces, iron weapons began to replace the bronze. Iron weapons became predominate from 1200-1000 BCE, gradually replacing bronze weapons throughout the Mesopotamian area. Around 900 BCE the iron sword was introduced in West Asia.

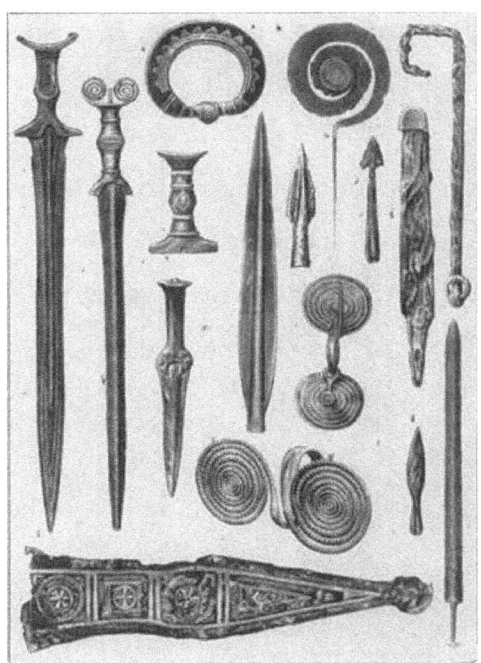

19th Century illustration of Bronze-Age weapons.

The earliest sword found thus far in China (Taiwan) was an iron sword some 60 centimeters long (approximately 24 inches in length) uncovered in the grave of an 18-year-old male, which has been dated to 1500 BCE. Most likely, the young man was a warrior of some reputation or a member of a royal family since iron weapons were regarded as extremely precious at that time.[5]

This period in time was one characterized by many technological and social changes. Among these changes was a change in weaponry. As Stuart Piggott wrote "In the Aegean, fighting tactics had rather rapidly changed from the use of the dagger to that of the rapier or sword, supported by spears and with shields or body-armour as a defence. In continental Europe we can see the same trend, with the early daggers becoming the rapiers and short-swords of the middle and the long-swords of the end, of the second millennium." [6]

Another breakthrough occurred around 1500 BCE when, according to Piggott, "a new type of slashing sword unknown at that time in the Mediterranean world; heavy, and with its hilt securely fastened by a flanged tang. It became immensely popular, particularly in the north, and then, between 1250 and

---

[5] "Taiwan's earliest sword to date uncovered in Tainan" in *Taiwan Headlines*, www.taiwanheadlines.gov.tw/fp.asp?xItem=59179&CtNode=8, 1/22/07

[6] Piggott, Stuart. *Ancient Europe from the beginnings of Agriculture to Classical Antiquity*. Chicago: Aldine Publishing Company 1965, 145.

1200, such swords, or copies of them, suddenly appear in the Aegean world." [7]

While viewed as inferior to bronze swords, as well as crude, iron swords were stronger and could be mass-produced. Entire armies could be outfitted with identical weapons. The iron sword spread the use of the longer bladed weapon that were now capable of stabbing and slashing. The use of the dagger and axe as the principal weapons of battle was ending, albeit slowly. The coexistence of the iron sword with the older technologies continued for centuries.

Sword sheaths did not appear until approximately 2000 BCE and were widespread by 1000 BCE. The necessity of the sheath to protect the blade as well as the swordsman became apparent with the use of iron blades. The first sheaths were made of wood, copper and bronze and were followed by leather sheaths. While the leather sheath protected the blade, it also kept the edge keen that was an issue with the wood and metal sheaths previously made that had dulled the blade.

The Assyrian Empire was well established by 665 BCE. The Assyrians are credited with the development of the sword, as it is known today. Their use of iron weapons assured the Assyrians of their desires for conquest.

---

[7] Ibid., 146.

Babylonian relief showing a king slaying a lion with a double-edged sword, approximately 1350 BCE, British Museum. (Photo by Gary R. Varner)

The Roman army preferred the short sword, or gladius, which was a commonly made sword in the third to first millennium BCE. "Borrowed" from the Spanish, these short swords were made for upward stabbing at close quarters, which became a fighting technique perfected by the Roman army. The gladius is responsible for swordplay being incorporated as an important part of the infantry tactics of that age. [8]

---

[8] Regan, Paula, ed. *Weapon: A Visual History of Arms and Armor.* London: DK Books 2006, 10.

By 500 BCE, the long sword had become the preferred weapon of battle. It is interesting to note that iron weapons had not advanced from the 7the century BCE until Medieval times. While the Romans often mocked the weapons of the barbarian tribes that they fought, Piggott notes, "even in the early centuries A.D. their untempered tools were technologically not superior to those of the barbarians." [9]

A further technological advancement was made by the Chinese around the time of Jesus with the development of steel.

Chinese metal smiths found that by adding small amounts of carbon to iron during the smelting process steel could be produced which by far was the most superior metal yet for weapons manufacture.

Around 900 CE a new form of blade was introduced that was not only stronger but also sharper—the Damascus blade. These swords, actually sabers, were legendary. The technique used to forge these weapons was lost in the 18th century and until recently; it was believed that "a special alloy and a secret forging process" were instrumental. [10] The Damascus blade, according to Wills, "produced a blade that met the two most important criteria for an effective, reliable sword—hardness, which allowed the blade to be sharpened to a razor like edge, and

---

[9] Piggott, op cit., 186.
[10] Wills, op cit., 92.

flexibility, which kept the blade from breaking when struck against an opponent's weapon." [11]

The Damascus blade has been thought to be made from a metal called "wootz steel". Wootz is an alloy used in Indian metalsmithing since as early as 200 BCE. Significant advanced research conducted in 2006 by the Dresden University in Germany discovered the true nature of the Damascus blade.

Using an electron microscope, Dresden University scientists determined that the famed Damascus blade was forged using nano-technology. The blade's microstructure was formed with nano-metre-sized tubes similar to the carbon nanotubes used in modern technological applications. [12] Evidently, the wootz steel contained "transition-metal impurities" that, at high temperatures, "helped cementite wires to form" which created the strength in the blades. [13]

It should be noted that the true Damascene blade, referred to as "crucible-steel," did not reach Europe until the 11th century CE.

Swords of the Celts

When we speak of the Celts, we are making broad statements about a people and culture that spread from Asia to

---

[11] Ibid.
[12] Sanderson, Katharine. "Sharpest cut from nanotube sword." news@nature.com 15 November 2006.
[13] Ibid.

the British Isles. A culture and people nevertheless united in their art, language, mythology and religious beliefs. They had perhaps one of the most artistic cultures in their time as well, decorating not only items of utilitarian nature, but their weapons, clothing and bodies as well.

Early Celtic swords were round tipped and erroneously were reported to be only useful as cutting weapons, they were considered inferior in their construction because they were said to bend after the first blow, or at least that was the opinion of the Roman Polybius. This can be explained by the dual construction of the blade. The cutting edge was formed of costly steel while the rest was made of a lesser, more pliable metal. It is also possible that Polybius saw swords that had been intentionally bent. It was a Celtic ritual to bend swords that they intended to "sacrifice" as votive offerings to the gods. There is a lack of historical evidence to suggest that the Celtic sword was less effective in battle than the swords of any rival.

True iron long swords were developed by the Celts during their La Téne period (500 BCE – 0 BCE). These swords were straight with the blades tapering to a rounded end. These swords were made for slashing from a chariot and are considered the direct ancestors of the typical knight's sword of the Middle Ages.

The La Téne culture was named for the shallows of Lake Neuchatel between the Rhine and Rhone Valleys. It was here between 1874 and 1881 that Swiss archaeologist Emile Vouge discovered a small Celtic military encampment with a stash of 100 swords, 200 spear-heads, axes, knives and chariot parts, among other non-domestic items. According to reports, all of the swords were found still in their scabbards. [14]

The Celts were warriors first and last. They lived and died for warfare and crushed the Roman army in 390 BCE and plundered the seat of the empire itself-Rome. Many of the Celtic weapons were made of bronze, as iron was a status item. Iron weapons were reserved for close combat using the sword and spear.

During the La Tène period, the Celts changed their daggers from the predominant double-edged form to a single edged knife resembling a butcher knife with a straight back slightly curving up to the point. The loss of the more highly decorative daggers of the earlier Hallstatt Culture to the plain, but functional daggers of the La Tène period may mean that the dagger had become less important to the Celts who regarded the sword as the superior weapon.

Historian Gerhard Herm wrote, "The swords of the La Téne era are evidence not only of a highly develop sense of formal

---

[14] Oakeshott, R. Ewart. *The Archaeology of Weapons.* Mineola: Dover Publications, Inc. 1996, 53.

beauty and functionalism, but also of changing tactical conceptions."[15] Earlier Hallstatt swords were short and obviously intended for stabbing actions while the La Téne sword was longer and functioned as a slashing weapon.

The Celts used both a heavy long sword and a short, one-handed sword. Celtic swords were commonly designed with an anthropomorphic hilt, looking much like a human being with the legs and arms forming part of the upper and lower guards. The purpose of these human-like hilts was not only decorative but to give the sword a particular magical charm to ensure protection.

"Iron swords," wrote Oxford Professor Barry Cunliffe, "in sheaths of iron, bronze, wood, or leather were the symbol of the warrior and as such were often personalized by elaborate decorations applied to the sheath or by stamps beaten into the blade." [16]

The importance that the warrior gave to his weapons is indicated by the giving of personal names to swords, spears and shields which, according to Mackenzie, may have originated in the ancient old stone-age Soultrean era.[17]

---

[15] Herm, Gerhard. *The Celts*. New York: St, Martin's Press, Inc. 1975, 126.
[16] Cunliffe, Barry. *The Ancient Celts*. Oxford: Oxford University Press 1997, 94.
[17] Mackenzie, Donald A. *Ancient Man in Britain*. London: Senate 1996, 51.

"Because a warrior's life depended on them," Martina Sprague wrote, "it was important for him to give an identity to his weapons and armor. The name a warrior gave to his sword created a bond between him and his weapon, gave him confidence in his abilities, and allowed him to believe he was invincible in battle." [18]

After the Celts began to utilize steel in their sword, making their blades became longer and stronger, with some sword lengths ranging from five to 6 feet in length. Hordes of screaming, blue-painted Celts running in attack and swinging swords as long or longer then they were must have been a terrible sight for any adversaries. However, they also contributed to the final defeat of the Celts by the Roman troops. The swords were too large for close combat; their weight was such that they became difficult for the Celtic warrior to wield effectively. The Roman infantry soldiers, after reinforcing their shields and body armor, were able to close ranks with the Celts and, by using their longer spears, disarm and slaughter them. Another Roman tactic was to simply step inside the enemy's "guard" so that the longer Celtic sword could not be swung in its intended slash movement.

The sword figured prominently in Celtic folklore. Manannán mac Lir, the son of the Lêr, the Poseidon of the Tuatha Dé

---

[18] Sprague, Martina. *Norse Warfare: The Unconventional Battle Strategies of the Ancient Vikings.* New York: Hippocrene Books, Inc. 2007

Danannan, carried a sword called "The Retaliator" which was said never to fail to slay.

The Tuatha De Danann reportedly brought four sacred objects of power to Ireland, all gifts of the gods:

1. The Sword of Nuadha
2. The Spear of Lugh
3. The Cauldron of the Daghdha, and
4. The Stone of Fal.

It was said that the Sword of Nuadha would slay any enemy once it was withdrawn from the scabbard, none could escape. The Spear of Lugh ensured victory. The Cauldron of the Daghdha continuously fed those who partook of its generosity, and the Stone of Fal would always give a sign, a human-sounding cry, when the rightful king was chosen to lead.

These four implement, according to R. J. Stewart, "all feature in Arthurian legend, and…are the implements of magical art to this day." [19]

The Roman Gladius and Pugio

Unfortunately, for the Celts, the Roman's had extraordinary discipline and tactical advantages over them. Even though the Celt warriors destroyed much of the Roman army in Britain, and even sacked Rome, they eventually were beaten down by the Roman soldier.

---

[19] Stewart, R.J. *Celtic Gods Celtic Goddesses.* London: Blandford 1990, 131.

The primary weapon of the Roman soldier was the *gladius,* or sword. The gladius was a double-edged weapon about two feet long and two inches wide. While the Celtic sword was a slashing weapon, the gladius was a stabbing implement and was used most successfully in close combat.

The Roman short-sword, a double-edged 20" blade with a diamond tip, became known as "the sword that conquered the world."

The *pugio* was the Roman dagger worn on the left side of the body and suspended from its own belt rather than from the sword belt. The pugio was most likely removed from Roman weaponry by the end of the 1st century.

The pugio was the standard issue to all Roman soldiers and was useful not only in battle but as a chopping blade for cooking. Tarassuk notes that the pugio was worn without its sheath on the chests of the Roman emperors "as a symbol of the *jus vitae et necis.*" Roman art shows this dagger also being worn by the imperial bodyguard and senior officials.

Burton notes that the pugio was very similar to daggers found in Egyptian tombs and may, in fact, have originated in Egypt. [20] He contradicts this statement earlier however by stating that after Rome invaded the Spanish Peninsula in their war with

---

[20] Burton, Richard F. *The Book of the Sword.* New York: Dover Publications, Inc. 1987, 257.

Carthage during the 1st century, they "adopted the Gladius Hispanus, including the pugio…" [21]

The Gladius Hispanus was a longer sword, being 34 inches long and 2 inches wide. Made of steel the blade was superior to the earlier Roman swords made of iron.

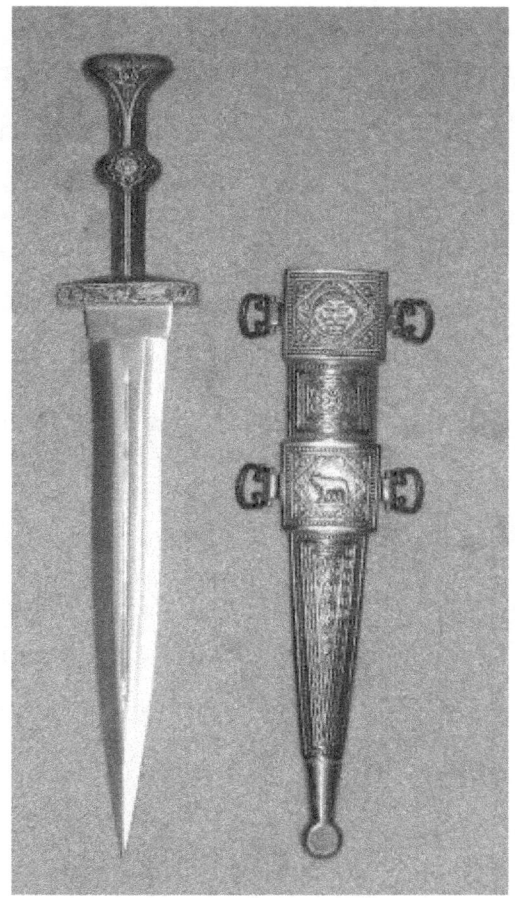

The Roman *pugio* dagger. (Author's collection)

---

[21] Ibid., 256

While the gladius was used as the main weapon of the infantry a longer sword called the *spatha* was introduced to the Roman cavalry around 100 CE. The spatha had blades 40 inches long and became the favored weapon of the Roman cavalry due to its reach, which was important for mounted combat from the horse or chariot.

After the 4th century, the double-edged spatha became the most used of Roman swords. The spatha evolved into the long bladed sword typically used by knights during the middle ages.

The Viking Sword

The Viking era between 750 CE and 1100 CE was the time of the final conflict between the converted Christian world and the remnants of the pagan cultures and traditions of the north.

The Vikings, like the Celts, were devoted to their weapons. A war god called by the Saxons *Saxnot* and the Germans Tiwaz was an ancestor of Odin and demanded extensive sacrifices. Some researchers believe that *Saxnot* originally meant "sword companion." [22] It was to Saxnot that the sword was dedicated in battle and sacrificed to.

---

[22] Davidson, H.R, Ellis. *Gods and Myths of the Viking Age*. New York: Bell Publishing Company 1981, 60.

Scandinavian law required every able-bodied male to possess weapons appropriate to his social status. Weapons of choice in Norway were the sword, ax, spear and shield. The Danes added an iron helmet to these as well.

To wealthy Vikings the Frankish sword was the preferred weapon. These swords had locally fitted hilts, which were decorated with gold, silver and copper.

Many Viking swords found over the years have the names of the makers stamped on the blades. Evidently, the Vikings utilized factories to produce vast numbers of weapons. The majority of swords have one of two names produced on the blade, either Ingelril or Ulfberht. Evidently, these were the names of the forgers or their factories. Other blades have been found with runic alphabets or religious verse stamped on them — again utilizing these techniques as protective charms.

According to Alan Baker, "The blades were double-edged, about 3 feet long and 4 inches wide at the base, tapering to a rounded tip. These weapons were used for slashing rather than thrusting, and were constructed by an ingenious method known as 'pattern welding.'" [23]

---

[23] Baker, Alan. *The Viking*. Hoboken: John Wiley & Sons, Inc. 2004, 38.

"Pattern welding" included twisting and plaiting together iron rods which were beaten into shape to form the central part of the blade which made it stronger, more pliable and harder to break. The next step was to weld a harder edge to the core of the blade, which left the pattern of the twisted rods visible on the blade itself.

It is remarkable that years after being in the earth, either dropped accidentally, intentionally left as votive offerings, or as part of grave goods, the pattern-welded blades were often burnished, resharpened, and used once again in battle. According to written records form the 11th century Muslim warriors often sought out and took swords from Scandinavian graves "because of their sharpness and excellence." [24]

Viking swords were between 31 and 39 inches long with most 35 ½ inches in length. Many of the hilts were decorated in geometric patterns, which also improved the grip.

After 900 CE, Viking swords were no longer made through the pattern welding technique but were constructed of a more flexible. Fine-quality steel. The

---

[24] Dvidson, Hilda Ellis. "Sword" in *Medieval Folklore.* Ed by Carl Lindahl, et al. Oxford: Oxford University Press 2002, 400.

advantage of this type of sword was that they were less point heavy (as the blade tapered to a point) and became easier to wield. These swords could not only be used to cut and slash but for thrusting.

The over-all effect of the Viking sword is one of perfection. "The marvelous swords of the Heroic Age," wrote Oakeshott, "with both blade and hilt works of lovely craftsmanship, often look ugly and clumsy, but the swords of the Vikings mostly have that austere perfection of line and proportion which is the essence of beauty." [25]

During the 9th and 10th centuries, the Vikings introduced the Frankish *scramasax* into their weaponry. This was considered the all-purpose knife of the Northmen. The blade of this knife ranged from 4 inches to as long as 20 inches. The longer versions were in reality short swords. The blades were normally straight and single-edged but it was considered "a sturdy knife. The blades were comparatively broad, suitable for dealing a heavy blow in fighting. The design permitted either a cut or a thrust, though the cutting actions seems to have been favoured." [26]

---

[25] Oakeshott, op cit., 134.
[26] Peterson, op cit., 10-11.

Many of these fighting knives have been found with the blades inscribed with runic alphabets and the names of the owner or manufacturer. Some scholars believe that *"scramasax"* means "a wound-making sword." This knife did not originate with the Vikings but they in effect made it their own. It continued in Viking use until the 12th century and continued as a popular weapon into 15th century England. According to Levine and Weland the scramasax "represents a transition between Iron Age daggers and more sophisticated fighting knives which we are familiar today." [27]

The Medieval Sword

After the Viking era, the sword had its first major change between the 11th and 13th centuries. The cross guard was added during this time. While some have stated that the lower guards, or the cross guards, were called *Quillons,"* Oakeshott disagrees. He wrote that the term "came into use only late in the sixteenth century; there is no scrap of evidence for its use during the Middle Ages, when it was always called the Cross... (or)...the hilt." [28] The

---

[27] Levine, Bernard & Gerald Weland. *Knives, Swords, Daggers.* New York: Barnes & Noble Books 2004, 110.
[28] Oakeshott, op cit.,203.

swords of this period were both single edged and double edged and were predominantly used as cutting weapons.

As Davidson wrote, "Medieval swords of good quality cut like razors, as is known by the terrible wounds left on the skeletons of men who fell in warfare...Both legs might be cut off by a single stroke..." [29] Other remains found from these battles include men who were cleft down the middle from head to saddle while mounted.

Continuing a long tradition, Medieval swords had both sides of the blade inscribed with religious invocations, such as BENEDICTUS DEUS MEUS, SANCTUS PETRNUS, or IN NOMINE DOMINI. [30]

As armor changed so did the sword, which became larger and heavier to penetrate the heavier armor. Sword length varied from 24 inches to over 6 feet. Medieval law restricted sword ownership to knights and the aristocracy, effectively ending most thoughts of rebellion among the peasant classes.

---

[29] Davidson op cit., 400.
[30] Oakeshott, op cit., 205.

Two examples of the "quillon." Left is the simple cross guard (13th century) and on the right is a more elaborate basket type (16th century). Both were designed to protect the hand and to keep it from sliding onto the blade during battle.

By the Late Middle Ages, after the 13th century, the sword had further changed. The handle became longer to allow both hands to grasp it with either the "hand-and-a-half" or the "two-handed" sword. In addition, other swords were designed to more effectively thrust and cut.

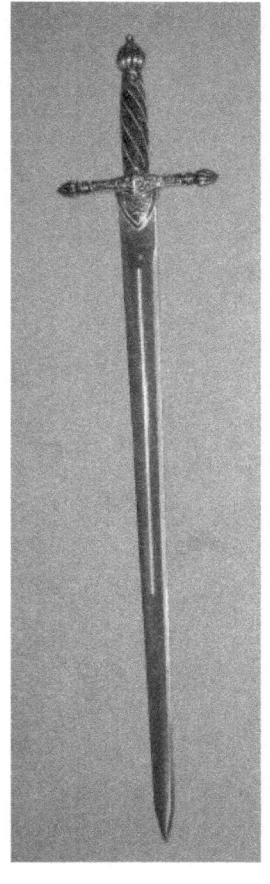

<A double-edged "hand-and-a-half" sword evolved from the Roman spatha into the Medieval sword used by the knighthood. Length 44". (Author's collection).

The "hand-and-a-half sword" pictured above was often referred to as the "bastard sword." The term was used for this particular weapon because the hand-and-a-half could be used in various ways. Descriptively these swords were long with a straight blade and rounded pommel. "The grip was sufficiently long," noted Levine and Weland, "so that it could be wielded by both hands in an overlapping grasp not dissimilar to that adopted when gripping a golf club." [31] This grip allowed the user to increase the swords impact regardless of the blow delivered. According to Levine and Weland, "Many people believe that the sword was one of

---

[31] Levine, Bernard and Gerald Weland. *Knives, Swords, Daggers*. New York: Barnes & Noble Books, Inc. 2004, 64.

the most effective and without doubt, the most versatile, long-bladed weapon ever developed." [32]

Decorated hilt and hand-guard of a "hand-and-a-half" sword.
(Author's collection)

The Renaissance

As armor changed from light chain mail to the heavy plate armor of the 15th and 16th centuries the sword changed from the short, lighter versions useful in close quarter battles to longer and heavier weapons called "long swords." These two handed swords were up to six feet in

---

[32] Ibid.

length and, while unable to pierce the heavy plate armor, were deadly and effective in penetrating between the plates.

These six-foot long swords were the longest of the European swords of the Renaissance and became synonymous with the mercenary troops from the Holy Roman Empire. These mercenaries were known as the Landsknecht. These mostly German troops were paid well but had to provide their own equipment, which meant that the majority used the less expensive pike, a 15-20 foot spear; a smaller, wealthy contingent used the two-handed sword. These were the best soldiers in the Landsknecht army. These long swords were not only impressive anti-personnel weapons but were also effective in dealing with enemy formations and in keeping pikes and halberds at a safe distance.

The German soldiers, which used the two-handed sword, were called "Doppelsöldners" and were given double pay. The pay was doubled because these soldiers always fought in the front lines. The two-handed sword was relatively light in comparison with its size but they still required considerable strength and expertise to use.

Another two-handed long sword that reached its zenith during the 15th and 16th centuries was the claymore. Originating in ancient Scotland, by the Renaissance it was widespread in its use. "Claymore" was derived from the Gaelic *claidheamh mór*, meaning "great sword."

The claymore was rarely decorated as it was first and foremost intended for battle. They were usually equipped with a quillon to prevent the users hand from sliding onto the blade due to the heavy force that was employed in their use.

It was common during the Renaissance for European sword blades to be decorated with religious icons, similar to the earlier bladed weapons of the Vikings.

A small sword often referred to as the weapon of gentlemen was the rapier. By the 15th century, this weapon was commonly used throughout Europe and, according to Regan, "would remain the premier gentleman's sword until the late 17th century." [33] The rapier had a long, thin blade. Today the rapier is used for fencing rather than battle. It was useful not as a battlefield weapon but for self-protection on the road, as a fashion accessory and for

---

[33] Regan, Paula, ed. *Weapon: A Visual History of Arms and Armor.* London: DK Books 2006, 110.

dueling purposes. The rapier was used mostly for thrusting or for parrying an enemy's weapon and had a stiff, triangular blade with blunt edges.

Normally held in the right hand, the rapier used in conjunction with a dagger held in the left hand could be a formidable weapon.

A 19th century Illustration of a rapier-dagger and an actual bone-handled example in the author's collection.

"The sword blade," wrote John Hayward, "was an object of international trade. The great majority were made in a few manufacturing centers and exported to all European countries, where they were equipped with hilts according to the local fashion." [34]

The Indian Sword & Other Blades of the East

The sword in India is as ancient as it is in Egypt. According to E. Jaiwant Paul, "the history of the sword can be traced back to the wondrous Indus valley civilization and its two main cities—Mohenjodaro and Harappa, which flourished from 3000 to 1500 B.C.—and coincides with the growth of the ancient civilizations of Egypt, Assyria and Babylon." [35]

The early swords of this region and period were all made of copper and were shorter than the swords that would evolve; in addition, the "antennae swords" of India, which date to around 2000 BCE, were cast of one piece of copper that comprised not only the blade but also the hilt. These weapons were called "antennae" due to the

---

[34] Hayward, J.F. *Swords & Daggers.* London: Victoria and Albert Museum/Her Majesty's Stationery Office 1963, 2.
[35] Paul, E. Jaiwant. *Arms and Armour: Traditional Weapons of India.* New Delhi: Lustre Press/Roli Books 2004, 17.

bifurcation of the hilt into two projections that stand at 45 degree angles to the base.

The handles of early Indian swords were crafted from the horns of the rhinoceros and the buffalo, elephant tusks or made from wood and bamboo. These types of hilts were commonly made in North African regions as well.

Around 200 CE the majority of swords were of the Roman type, the two edged short sword which became so effective in the Roman tactics of war.

Most of us are familiar with the long, curved saber traditionally associated with India. However, these weapons did not originate in India but were the result of the Mughal Empire that was established in Northern India during the 16th century. These swords, originally Persian, were curved, single-edged, tapering blades around 37 inches long and weighing approximately two pounds.

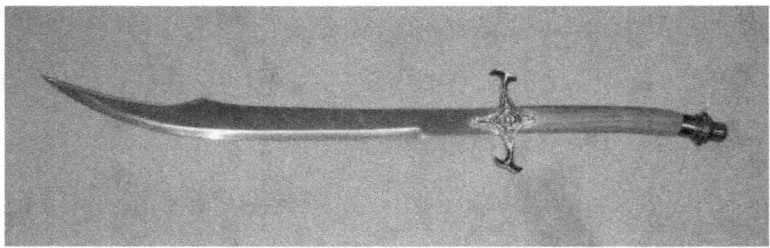

An Indian *shamshir,* or scimitar in the Old Turkish style. (Author's collection)

The from the thirteenth through the sixteenth centuries the Turks and Afghans controlled much of north-west India and the heavy Persian influence of their occupation resulted in a domination of the sword industry as well. "By the sixteen-hundreds," Paul notes "Indian swordsmiths and craftsmen had fully mastered the Persian techniques, so that it became difficult to say whether a weapon or piece of armour was Indian or Persian in origin."[36] This influence resulted in the Indian sword of the sixteenth century to be curved backward. The shamshir developed from these Persian forms.

The shamshir and its close relative, the *talwar*, were, according to historians, "near-perfection of form and function." [37] They were most suited for slashing and thrusting was more problematical. Both of these weapons were Islamic in tradition and spread throughout the area from the 16th to the 18th centuries.

While the soldiers of Islam utilized these swords, they were originally meant for the hunt.

Other Indian swords include the traditional Hindu sword, the *khanda*. The khanda is a straight bladed weapon,

---

[36] Paul, op cit., 41.
[37] Regan, op cit., 128.

approximately 35-39 inches in length and a little over two pounds in weight. While the shamshir was popularly made, the khanda continued in production for the use of the Indian princely courts. The very word *khanda* is an ancient Indian word that means "sword."

Rawson tells us "The essential character of this weapon is that it is a swung, slashing sword, with a good weight of blade metal at the tip, and an inconsiderable point. This is the earliest appearance of such a weapon in art..." [38] The khanda may have developed around the 2nd century CE although it continued to evolve throughout India's history into the 18th century.

Other blades found throughout India, Persia, Turkey, Armenia and Central Asia includes the *kard*. The kard is an Islamic knife which reached its peak in popularity in the 17th and 18th century. It had a straight blade averaging 8-16 inches in length. One of its characteristics is the sheath which was made of wood and covered in tooled leather.

---

[38] Rawson, P.S. *The Indian Sword.* New York: ARCO Publishing Company, Inc. 1968, 6.

The kard's point was sometimes thickened to enable it to pierce mail. [39]

Blades of Africa

A similar knife to the kard but from Southern Algeria is the example below. It is called a Bou Saddi, and has a decorated wooden hilt and red leather sheath.

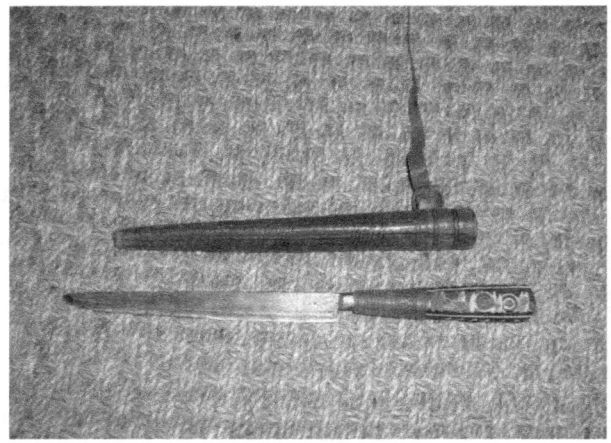

Bou Saddi, authors collection.

The Bou Saddi shown above also has unusual markings on the blade, which may indicate the makers "signature."

---

[39] Tarassuk, Leonid and Claude Blair, ed. *The Complete Encyclopedia of Arms & Weapons.* Crown Publishers, Inc. 1986, 291.

Bou Saddi blade markings.

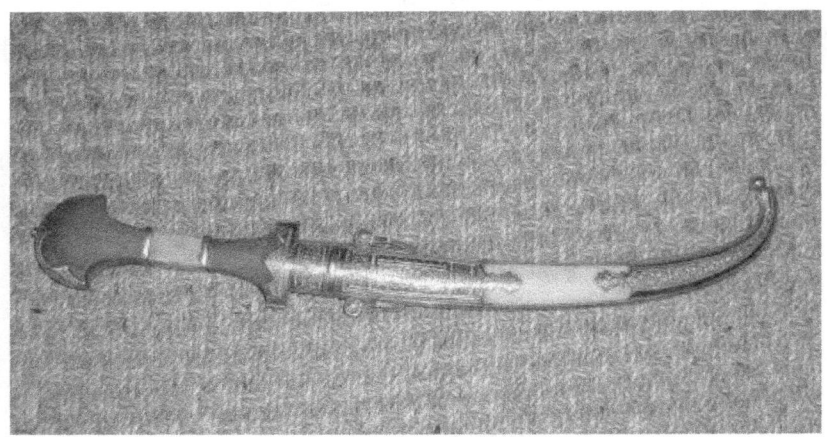

Moroccan "peacock" dagger with wooden grip and horn inlay. (Author's collection)

The weapon shown above is typical of the Moroccan *koummya* dagger with its elaborate sheath. It would have been worn from the owner's silk or leather sash. While decorative, it also served as an effective weapon as illustrated in the photograph on page 50 of a man on camelback fighting off an attack by a lion with his koummya.

Another blade carried by some Sudanese and Saharan tribes is the *kaskara*. Used into the present day, the kaskara dates back to the 10th century. While many local swordsmiths produced this weapon, eventually blades from Europe, including those from Solingen and Toledo, were imported to produce the kaskara. "The kaskara blade was straight," writes Tarassuk "between 31 and 39 inches long, double-edged, and with a central fuller." [40]

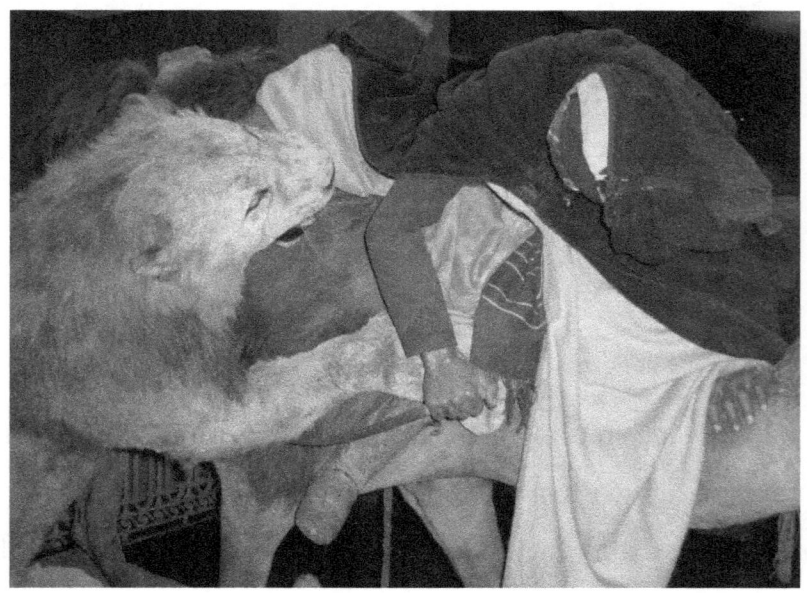

The koummya in action. Diorama in the Carnegie Museum of Natural History, Pittsburgh, PA. (Photo by the author)

---

[40] Tarassuk, op cit.,292.

Sudanese blades are of particular interest due to their unusual markings. There are two Sudan weapons of particular note. One is the "arm dagger" as shown below. On this particular weapon, a deeply carved "S" was engraved on both sides of the blade.

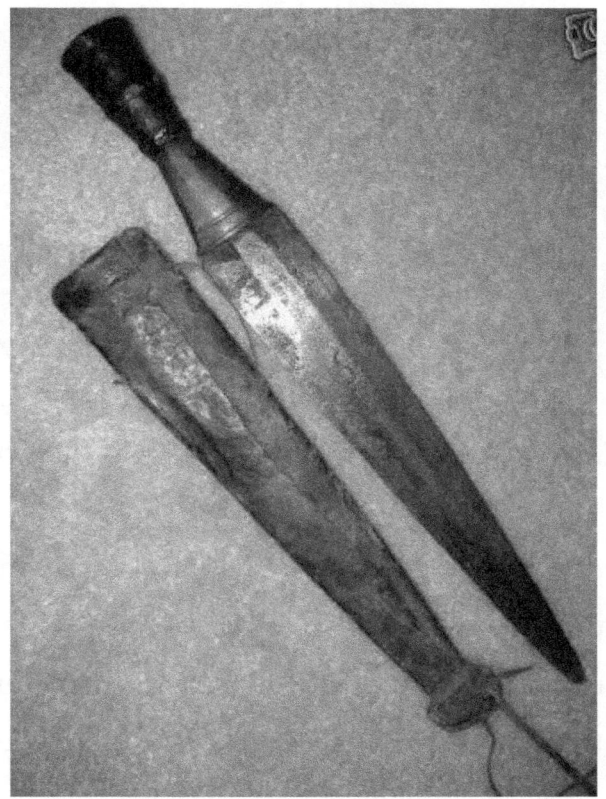

19th century Sudanese "arm dagger" (authors collection)

One researcher remarked, "Symbolized marks typically were intended to represent either material objects or often totemically associated animals or creatures. There seems of course a good possibility that the S shape may well represent obviously, the snake."

Such marks may also represent tribal identifiers used as brands on cattle and camels.

"S" symbol engraved on dagger blade. Totemic symbol or tribal marking?

Another possibility is that the "S" represents an unusual Sudanese weapon which is comprised of two reverse curved iron blades which were manufactured in Syria into the 20th century. If this is the case this dagger was possibly a ritual dagger and, as such, had a fairly elevated status in the tribal community.

Of course we cannot leave out the most important of African bladed weapons—the spear. Spears were not only effective weapons used on the hunt and in battle but were also status symbols and used for trade. In the past, five of the Ngbandi spears shown below could purchase a slave and 50 could buy a wife.

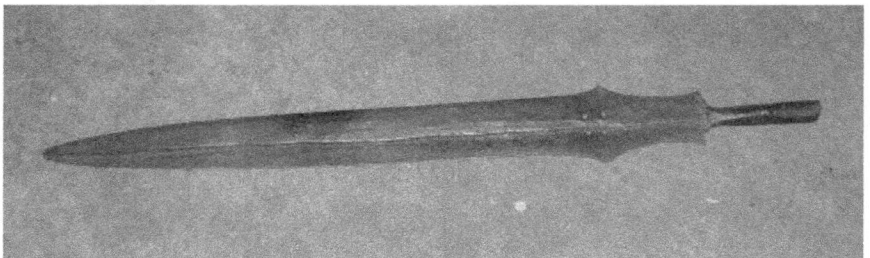

This 200 year old Ngbandi spear is 29 inches in length, 3 inches at its widest point. (Authors collection)

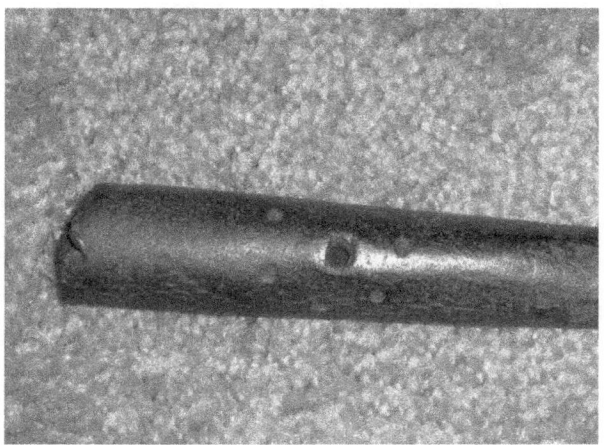

Many Ngbandi spears are decorated with a series of punches on the shaft. It is unknown if these marks are symbolic of some ritual purpose, have a numeric importance as a talisman or are the "finish" marks of the spear maker to indicate that the spear is "ready made."

Swords of the Orient

The Orient has had a long relationship with the sword. The Japanese samurai is certainly one of the most spiritually endowed weapons. John Yumoto wrote, "In ancient times it was well established that anything suitable as an offering to the gods had to possess three elements: purity, rarity, and value. The sword was believed to have all of these characteristics, and it was a not uncommon practice to give one as a votive offering." [41]

The samurai sword, long associated with the Japanese elite warrior, was perhaps the finest blade ever made. In existence for over 1200 years, the samurai sword's "success was due to the combination of a hard cutting edge with a softer, resilient core and back." [42]

The Japanese warrior did not utilize a shield but instead blocked blows with the back of his sword. According to John H. Lienhard, Professor Emeritus of

---

[41] Yumoto, John M. *The Samurai Sword: A Handbook.* Rutland: Charles E. Tuttle Company 1958, 11.
[42] Regan, op cit., 120.

Mechanical Engineering and History at the University of Houston, the blade of the samurai sword was "heated, folded and beaten—over and over—until the blade is formed by 32,768 layers, forge-welded to one another. Each layer is a hundred thousandth of an inch thick...The result is an obsidian-hard blade with willow-like flexibility." [43]

For some reason it is only the Japanese sword that has attained mythic stature in weaponry. The Chinese sword, of which many are quite beautifully made, have straighter blades but do not have the spiritual or mythic association attached to them as the Japanese sword does.

The samurai class emerged in 1185 when the shogunate gained ascendancy in Japan but the sword did not become the dominate samurai weapon until the 13th century when warfare became highly individualistic and ritualized.

The samurai warrior ceased to exist after 1868 when the ruling Tokugawa-clan shoguns were overthrown by the imperial court in Kyoto. According to Fuller and Gregory, "Among the first to suffer was the privileged samurai class. Compulsory wearing of swords by samurai was made optional in 1871, as was the cutting of hair. Withdrawn,

---

[43] Lienhard, John H. "The Samurai Sword"
http://www.uh.edu/engines/epi1384.htm 3/2/2007

too, was a samurai's right to kill a commoner for any insult—real or imaginary." [44]

By 1876, the samurai class ceased to exist after the Meiji Restoration and no blade forged after that time can be called "samurai."

The Modern Era

The modern era is defined, for this work anyway, as the 19th century onward. The sword continued to be used as a weapon of battle but eventually "evolved" into the bayonet that was used not only on the end of a rifle but also as a short sword in close combat.

By the end of the Napoleonic Wars, the dominance of the sword as a fighting weapon was on the decline. However, the saber continued to be used extensively by mounted warriors until World War I.

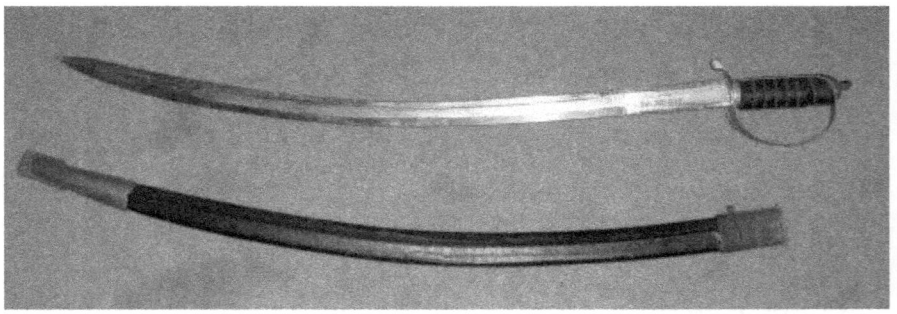

---

[44] Fuller, Richard and Ron Gregory. *Military Swords of Japan 1868-1945*. London: Arms and Armour Press 1986, 7.

Sabers similar to this US Civil War weapon shown above were the most common bladed weapon from the 1700's until World War I. (Author's collection)

Trench warfare was disastrous in many ways but primarily for the troops ordered to advance with fixed bayonets, they were machine-gunned down by enemy forces. Bayonets at this time were long bladed in order to give the soldier additional reach but, according to fighters at the time, "were more use for opening cans than for combat." [45] Or, according to Canadian troops so equipped in World War I, "useless for anything except toasting bread over campfires." [46]

The bayonet shown below was fitted to the .303 Short Magazine Lee Enfield rifles, which remained in service for over fifty years.

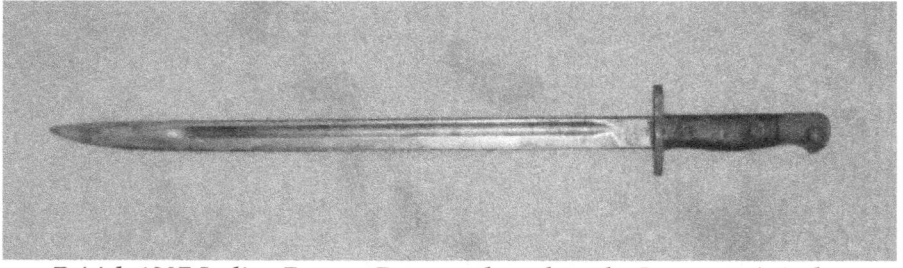

British 1907-Indian Pattern Bayonet, based on the Japanese Arisaka bayonet. The typical WWI weapon, 22" in length. (Author's collection)

---

[45] Regan, op cit., 284
[46] Willis, op cit., 180

The Japanese throughout World War II used swords as part of their military arsenal, using ancient samurai swords passed down along family lines or civilian weapons that had been modeled on the samurai. It has been estimated that over one million swords were carried by Japanese troops until they were removed from their possession around 1946. [47]

Even in modern times, weapons of war reflect an earlier time. The Nazis modeled their SA and SS fighting daggers from 16th century Swedish designs. The fighting knife, however, became a standard issue to all troops around the world and is still a contemporary weapon—even, as Peterson says, "American astronauts now carry big all-purpose knives with fighting guards on their trips through space." [48]

---

[47] Fuller and Gregory, op cit., 101.
[48] Peterson, Harold L. *Daggers and Fighting Knives of the Western World.* Mineola: Dover Publications, Inc. 1968, 80.

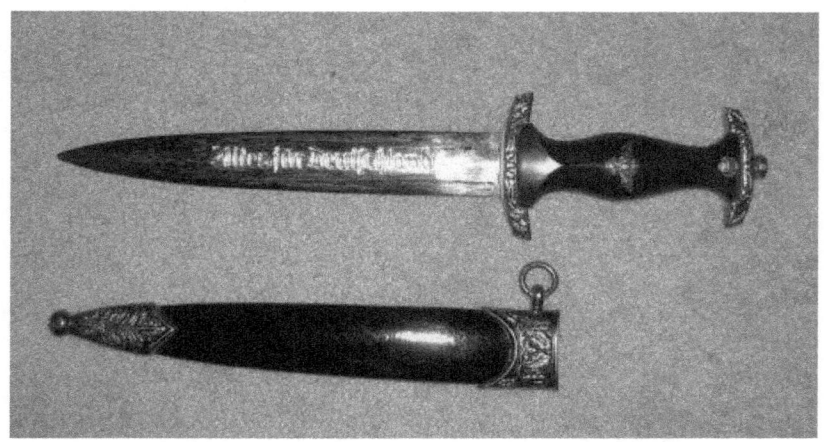

Nazi SA Dagger modeled after the Swiss holbein dagger from the 16th century. The inscription on the blade reads, "Allies fur Deutschland". (Author's collection) The SA Dagger, similar to this one, was used extensively in the 1933 street battles, which brought Hitler to power.

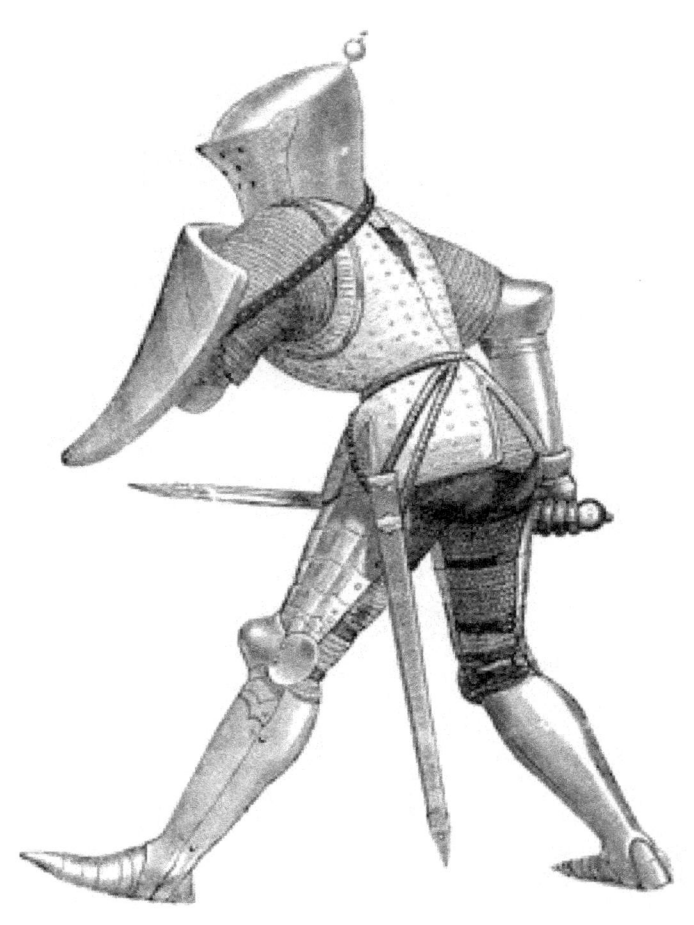

Chapter Two
The Sacred & Mythic Sword

The sword, like no other weapon, figures prominently in folklore and legend. The sword symbolizes purity, intelligence and knowledge, justice and divine truth and wisdom. It has also been used as a tool of savagery. Like everything in the universe, it has a dual nature of both good and evil. In many ancient cultures the sword, like the axe, became the impersonation of deity. The ancient Babylonian goddess Ishtar, for example, was called both the sword or lightning of heaven.

The sword obtained its ceremonial purpose due to the various sword cults that evolved in Japan and during the Crusades. The sword is one of the three sacred treasures of Japan, the other two being the mirror and the jewel.

In India, the sword was representative of god. According to Sir James Frazer, young girls who had been dedicated to "Tamil temples" were "formally married, sometimes to the idol, sometimes to a sword, before they enter their duties; from which it appears that they are often, if not regularly, regarded as wives of the god." [49] In Buddhist tradition the sword is a symbol of

---

[49] Frazer, Sir J.G. *Adonis: A Study in the History of Oriental Religion. The Thinker's Library, No. 30.* London: Watts & Co. 1932, 45.

wisdom "that cuts through the veil of ignorance and obscuration." [50]

Likewise, the sword in Indian mythology was certainly an object of veneration. Hopkins noted, "Brahman created Asi, the Sword, as a divine being to protect men, and gave it to Rudra, who gave it to Viṣṇu, who gave it to Merīci. Merīci passed it over to the Seers...." [51] It eventually was passed to Indra and then to Manu, the lawgiver. The Seers, referred to as "saints," were gods in their own right. While there were 82,000 Seers, there were seven who were considered leaders and who visited man in peace and war. While said to create worlds, they also acted to protect humankind and by obtaining Asi, the Sword, they were able to combat evil.

The Asi, according to the sage Vaishampáyana, "was a superior weapon, introduced especially and separately by Brahma…" [52] Burton relates, "This 'Sword-god' appeared on the summit of the Himálayas shaking earth's foundations and illuminating the sky." [53]

The asi is also representative of Manjushri, the Bodhisattva of wisdom in Tibetan Buddhism. In Buddhist lore, Manjushri is

---

[50] Beer, Robert. *The Handbook of Tibetan Buddhist Symbols.* Boston: Shambhala Publications 2003, 123
[51] Hopkins, E. Washburn. *Epic Mythology.* Delhi: Motilal Banarsidass 1986, 176.
[52] Burton, Richard F. *The Book of the Sword.* New York: Dover Publications, Inc. 1987, 214.
[53] Ibid.

believed to have created the Kathmandu valley in Nepal by cutting through the surrounding mountain ranges with his sword, "moonderiding." By cutting through the mountains, Manjushri emptied a large lake that had filled the valley.

This sword of wisdom was also used to destroy demons and evil deities. Beer describes the sword of wisdom:

"The wisdom sword is fashioned of blue iron, with a coiling flame twisting around its double-edged blade and emanating as a blaze of wisdom-fire around its tip. Its handle is fashioned of gold, and sealed with a five-pronged half-*vajra* as a pommel." [54] The swords double-edged blade evidently symbolizes the unity of truth, the perfection of wisdom and wisdom-awareness.

Other important bladed-weapons of Buddhism include the Scorpion-Hilted Sword, which is regarded as "an extremely wrathful weapon" wielded by demons and gods responsible for plague and pestilence. This blade is made of meteoric materials and is believed to be both violent in nature and indestructible.

The gods of ancient Egypt were commonly associated with the blade. Burton wrote "The god Anhar, or Shu, is 'Lord of the Scymitar,' Horus, as a hawk-headed mummified deity, is seated holding two swords. Amen-Ra, Lord of Hab, is a 'great god Ramenma, "Lord of the Sword." [55]

---

[54] Beer, op cit., 124
[55] Ibid., 152.

In 1884 when Burton's book was first published, the "Sword-god" was still the supreme deity of the Himalayas and fought to "free the world from the Asuras or mighty daemons." [56]

Another deity, Agni who was "all the gods" was said to constitute "the 'asterism and divinity of the sword.'" [57]

The sword was a very important item to ancient people, often taking on mythic characteristics and proportions. It was one of the most frequently ritually deposited items found in the rivers and lakes of Europe and Britain. Both war trophies and personally deposited swords by warriors they were willingly given to the gods and goddesses beginning in the Bronze Age and continuing into the Iron Ages.

Historian and archaeologist Ralph Merrifield wrote, "The practice of depositing valuables, particularly weapons, in watery places extends far back into the Bronze Age, and Colin Burgess has suggested that there was a fundamental religious change in the Middle Bronze Age, when the old gods of sky and earth, whose great sanctuaries were on the Wessex uplands, were displaced in favour of water deities, possibly as a result of climate deterioration." [58]

---

[56] Ibid., 214.
[57] Ibid., 105.
[58] Merrifield, Ralph. *The Archaeology of Ritual and Magic.* New York: New Amsterdam Books 1987, 24.

Some of the worshippers, however, valued their weapons more as articles of war than as religious offerings. Five bone daggers created in imitation of Bronze Age daggers then in use, have been found in the Thames River. Two of the carved daggers were made to appear to be sheathed. As Merrifield indicates, these daggers "were made as votive substitutes for metal weapons which were too valuable to be sacrificed. ...Substitutes of this kind have always been considered legitimate in ritual; for the gods and the dead need only the essence or 'soul' of the offering..." [59] thus avoiding an economic and material loss that could not be replaced.

By 1965, historian Ronald Hutton notes, 34 Viking swords had been discovered in English rivers, "and the relative absence of other kinds of hardware suggests that these had been offerings and not accidental losses." [60]

Weapons were not only deposited in the lakes, rivers or bogs of Europe but also on land. A find of Bronze Age axes, spearheads and swords were found in a pit in Monmouthshire, England in 2006. They were buried in a small pit "as a ritual gift to the pagan gods of the time." [61] Dated between 1,000 and 800 BCE, the swords had been broken prior to their burial.

---

[59] Ibid., 25.
[60] Hutton, Ronald. *The Pagan Religions of the Ancient British Isles*. Oxford: Blackwell 1993, 283.
[61] "3,000-year-old tools to museum". BBC News, 11/20/2006

By no means were such offerings confined to Britain. The peat bogs in Scandinavia were also found to have large deposits of weapons deposited. Many times these offerings reflected the total annihilation of an opposing force, their weapons and armor taken by the victors and deposited in the bogs and lakes in thanks to the gods. One deposit excavated at Illerup in 1950 was composed of the swords, shields and armor of seventy warriors. The weapons had been burned with their owners bodies but removed from the ashes, deliberately bent and dented and then reflects the results of the spoils of battle from around 400 CE. [62]

Similar deposits of votive offerings occurred in Denmark from the 2nd to the 6th century CE. Davidson writes, "The explanation given in literature is that they did this in order to placate the god of battle…in the fulfillment of a vow once victory had been won." [63]

Early twentieth-century writer Helene Guerber notes that the sword was so important and sacred to the Norse that "it became customary to register oaths upon it." [64]

Swords in particular appear to be weapons most commonly associated with the supernatural. Underworld elves, dwarves, or

---

[62] Davidson, H.R. Ellis. *Gods and Myths of the Viking Age.* New York: Bell Publishing Company 1964, 56.
[63] Ibid.
[64] Guerber, Helene A. *Myths of the Norsemen.* New York: Barnes & Noble 2006, 92.

64

the famous underworld smithy, Weland (or Wayland) reportedly forged many of the swords used by heroes.

By 1150 CE, the sword had acquired the symbolism that would exist with it for the rest of time. The Crusades had laid waste the Holy Land but in doing so had given the sword its "final touch of Christian sanctity." [65]

The Church adapted the Viking sword-form and made it holy. The cross guard of the sword was regarded as a protection against sin and a weapon against the forces of evil and the enemies of Christ. Oakeshott wrote, "Its two-edged blade stood for truth and loyalty, one side for the strong who persecute the weak and the other for rich oppressors of the poor." [66] Of course, history shows very vividly that this symbolism was not based in reality.

"The coming of Christianity," wrote historian Vesey Norman, "may have taken away some of the sword's magic, but replaced this with its own religious significance." [67] The religio-magic significance was enforced by:

- Oaths taken on sword hilts, the cross-shaped hilt adding to the religious symbolism;

---

[65] Oakeshott, R. Ewart. *The Archaeology of Weapons*. Mineola: Dover Publications Inc. 1996, 200.
[66] Ibid., 200.
[67] Norman, Vesey. *The Medieval Soldier*. South Yorkshire: Pen & Sword Books Limited 2006, 238.

- Christian relics placed inside the sword's pommel to give the owner the added protection of the saints; and
- Inscriptions made on the blades to give the warrior supernatural protection and power.

Many times warriors would attach magical or religious charms to their swords to increase their chances of survival and to give a boost to the strength of the weapon.

Folklore says that one effective weapon against Fairies is the sword; in fact any iron weapon is useful. Supposedly, a sword or knife stuck in the door of a Fairy dwelling will prevent the door from being closed until the intruder (the sword or knife owner) willingly exits.

In Indian religious tradition, the sword represents Kālī, the Dark Lady of the World. "In one right hand she carries the sword, the symbol of physical extermination and spiritual decision; this sword cuts through error and ignorance, the veil of individual consciousness." [68] The sword is also one of the emblematic implements of Shiva.

Excalibur, Durendal, Gram, Balmung, Dhami, Cloud Cluster…all names of powerful weapons. Weapons belonging to hero's from Japan to the Arab world, to ancient Britain to the Norse countries—all swords of mythic proportions.

---

[68] Zimmer, Heinrich. *Myths and Symbols in Indian Art and Civilization.* Ed by Joseph Campbell. Princeton: Princeton University Press/Bollingen Series VI 1972, 214.

< 16th Century German sword with religious charm inscribed on the blade. >

"The sword was an aristocratic weapon," notes historian Hilda Davidson, "associated with kings and heroes and used against human and supernatural foes…" [69]

The warrior's sword was often buried with him but could also be passed down from one generation to another with stories of heroic battles growing with each passing. As Davidson wrote, "the efficiency and beauty of famous swords was a favorite subject for poets and storytellers." [70]

The sword is emblematic of magic as is seen in the legends of many of the swords mentioned above. As previously indicated, many of these swords of heroes were forged by the underworld dwarves or by the underworld smithy, Weland. Weland was a giant, an underworld being who forged the finest weapons and

---

[69] Davidson, Hilda Ellis. "Sword" in *Medieval Folklore: A Guide to Myths, Legends, Tales, Beliefs, and Customs.* Oxford: Oxford University Press 2000, 399.
[70] Ibid.

who reportedly raised many of the megalithic ruins still in existence throughout Europe.

"Wayland's Smithy" is located in Oxfordshire, England not far from the famous Uffington White Horse. Legends of Wayland and his smithy have survived in this area for over a thousand years even though the legend may have originated in the Germanic countries in the stories of Volundr. Legend says that the smithy was located in a megalithic tomb chamber on the Ridegway not far from the chalk figure of the Uffington Horse.

The spot said to be the smithy site was recorded in 855 CE in the Berkshire Charter as *Welands smidde.* References to Weland/Wayland/Weiland have survived in Old English poetry. He is mentioned in Beowulf as the "maker of a fantastic coat of mail" and by other poets as the creator of great bladed weapons. [71]

According to Christopher Fee, professor of English at Gettysburg College, we have a paradox in Wayland. "…his name appears in a number of Old English texts and representations of him appear in various artistic contexts, quite often in combination with Christian motifs; here is a god who was clearly known and revered in pagan and early Christian England (as well as in the rest of the Germanic world), whose name has remained current in English literature almost until the

---

[71] Fee, Christopher R. *Gods, Heroes, & Kings: The Battle for Mythic Britain.* Oxford: Oxford University Press 2001, 62.

present day...it has been argued persuasively that Weland the Smith was so well known, and so many tales accrued about him, that allusions to him were often made without any attempt to flesh out the all too familiar stories." [72] Thus, we have only the barest outline concerning the details about the smithy and his legend.

"...weapons of quality," Fee notes, "were sometimes designated 'the work of Weland' by the Anglo-Saxons."[73] Weland's story is intricately linked with other myths and symbolism. His importance to ancient people cannot be underestimated but it must have been tremendous even if we are left in the dark concerning any of the true details.

"Ancient giant figures like...Weland may appear as a hero, a giant or a supernatural smith and remain a shadowy power in folklore for centuries...These outstanding figures," wrote Davidson, "from the myths of people who grew apart from one another but must once have been closely linked have remained recognizable, and still reflect something of the force which they must once have possessed in the minds of men." [74]

Good smiths were exceedingly sought after and were often thought to have the aid of supernatural forces and "special

---

[72] Ibid.
[73] Ibid., 160.
[74] Davidson, H.R. Ellis. *Myths and Symbols in Pagan Europe: Early Scandinavian and Celtic Religions.* Syracuse: Syracuse University Press 1988, 216.

secrets." Such secrets included "the virtues of certain liquids for quenching the hot iron, varying from the water of certain rivers to the urine of a red-haired boy or the juice of radishes mixed with earthworms." [75]

The sword has figured prominently in Biblical stories usually depicted as a flaming sword wielded by angels. These accounts may be considered exaggerations of true blades. "Flaming swords," also called "flamboyant," "Floberge," or "flamberg" are blades made with a serpentine or waved edges. Regan notes that while the blade is attractive, it "made little difference to its cutting qualities." [76] Similar bladed weapons from Java and Indonesia are commonly referred to as "kris" or "keris" blades. Kris blades are still commonly used and made in Malaysia and Indonesia. Each kris is considered a living thing with its own soul, capable of bringing either good or bad luck. They were also thought to have the capability to act on their own, jumping out of their scabbards to engage a perceived enemy.

The kris, originating in the 14th century, is always formed of three layers of steel or iron with thinner layers fitted between and then twisted or beaten into shape. Most often, the kris was decorated with engravings of demons or dragons.

The kris was intended for three purposes:

---
[75] Davidson, op cit, 399.
[76] Regan, Paula, editor. *Weapon: A Visual History of Arms and Armor.* London: DK Publishing 2006, 102.

1. A thrusting weapon

2. A religious cult object, and

3. An executioner's weapon.

However, it also became an item of apparel and most every Indonesian/Malayan male would wear on at his side.

According to martial arts expert, Ramon Villardo [77] the kris "is regarded as man's tutelary spirit and a means of communicating with one's ancestors."

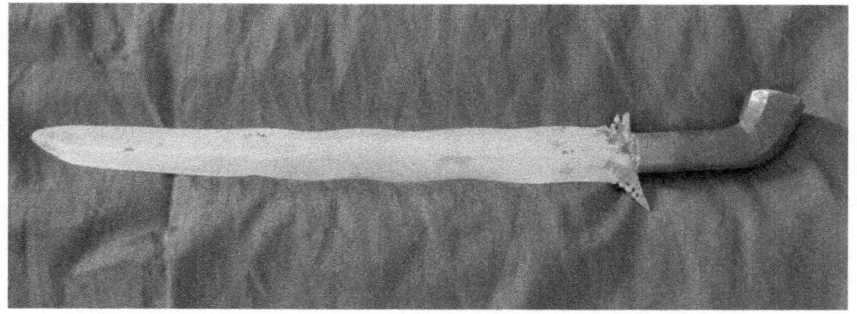

A hand-made Malay kris ca. 1950 (author's collection)

Some of the mythology and folklore associated with the kris is that some people have said that they have seen water drawn from the blade—more than likely due to the curved or "wavy" nature of the blade itself. Villard also writes "The very act of death could be performed by merely pointing the weapon at the intended victim…It is also believed to be able to rattle its own

---

[77]Villardo, Ramon. "Kris daggers and swords of Indonesia and the Philippines." http://www.bakbakan.com/kris.htm. 3/7/07

scabbard to call notice and warn its owner of an impending danger..." [78]

While others have said the kris is capable of bringing either good or bad Villardo states "It is a firm belief that the powers of religion and of the kris could only be manifested for good purposes."

However, anecdotal information would appear to present a different picture. Some have been linked to a series of violent deaths, failed businesses and the ability to grant prophetic powers. Extreme care is warranted for those possessing the kris and unusual preservation measures have been taken by some to ensure that the knife remains docile and protected. Some of these techniques are:

- The kris are kept in boxes in chests of drawers
- All kris are laid out in a horizontal fashion
- The kris blade is kept oiled (the oil consisting of 50% medicinal paraffin, 45% sandalwood oil and 5% kenanga oil [*Canangium odoratum*] a fragrant plant which is one of the principal ingredients of Chanel No. 5)
- The kris is kept wrapped in plastic
- All kris must be allowed to "breath" so that the spirit of the blade does not suffocate.

---

[78] Ibid.

Additional anecdotal information is that the kris will move on its own from place to place in the house—it is a truly living being to those familiar with the weapon.

A contributor to the English journal, *Notes and Queries*, wrote "Ancient swords were frequently 'flamboyant,' or with waved edges; more especially those used for purposes of state…Indeed, 'flaming swords,' as they were called, were worn down to the time of our Charles II, and perhaps later." [79]

Stories of miraculous swords such as Excalibur may be based on fact. A true "Sword in the Stone" exists and is still found in an ancient abbey in Tuscany, just 30 km south of Siena.

According to legend, Galgano Guidotti, born in 1148, "was said to have been an arrogant and dissolute young man who became a knight after seeing a vision of the Archangel Michael. Later, during a second dream, Galgano was led by St. Michael across a narrow bridge over dangerous waters, to a wonderful field filled with flowers and thence through a dark underground passage into a round building where he met twelve individuals…and shown a book that he was not able to read…and had a vision of God's majesty." [80] As Galgano

---

[79] Smith, W.J. Bernhard. "'The Sword Flamberg'" in *Notes and Queries*, Vol.3 (76) April 12, 1851, 292.
[80] Garlaschelli, Luigi. "The *Real* Sword in the Stone", in *Skeptical Inquirer*, March/April 2006.

continued on his trip home, his horse suddenly stopped at a place that Galgano recognized to be the same in his vision.

"Here, on a small hill named Montesiepi," the legend goes, "he thrust his sword into a rock — where it remains to this day — giving up a life of war and violence for that of a hermit and adoring the upside-down sword which resembled a Christian cross." [81]

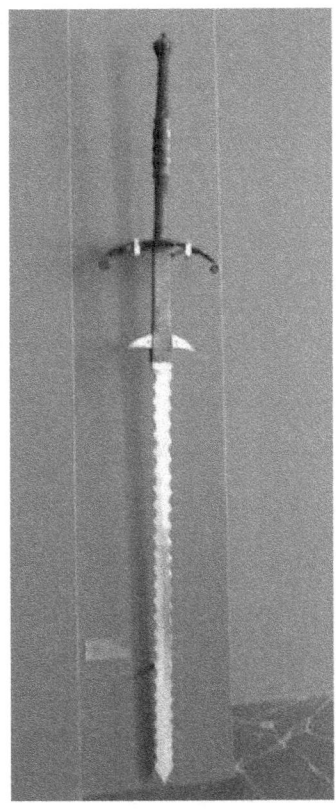

16th Century Flamberg, Dresden, Zwinger-Museum.

---

[81] Ibid.

Galgano died a year later at the age of 33. The sword is still hilt deep in the stone at the little abbey in Tuscany. Its age has been validated through thermoluminescence analysis conducted in 2001 by Luigi Garlaschelli a research chemist from the Universitá di Pavia and further testing is underway. Galgano was later sainted even though this sword in the stone is his only reported miracle. It is very possible that the story of St. Galgano is the bases for the legends of King Arthur and the legendary Sword in the Stone. It has been noted that Galgano phonetically is very close to "Galvano" which is Italian for "Galwin", or Gawain, the famous knight of the Round Table.

Dr. Garlaschelli, using themoluminescence, determined that the round building located on the abbey grounds which was so prominent in Galgano's vision, was constructed around 985 CE. The sword is a typical weapon of the late 12th century and has been classified as an Xa-type sword, that of a medieval sword. He notes "Written and pictorial records confirm the actual presence of a sword in that stone since at least 1270 A.D." [82]

Dr. Garlaschelli also notes that the date of this sword-in-the stone would correspond with the legend of King Arthur, also written in the 12th century. It is very possible that the legend of this sword was the basis for the lore surrounding Excalibur.

---

[82] Ibid.

The Sword in the Stone of St. Galgano, Tuscany.
(Photo courtesy Dr. Luigi Garlaschelli)

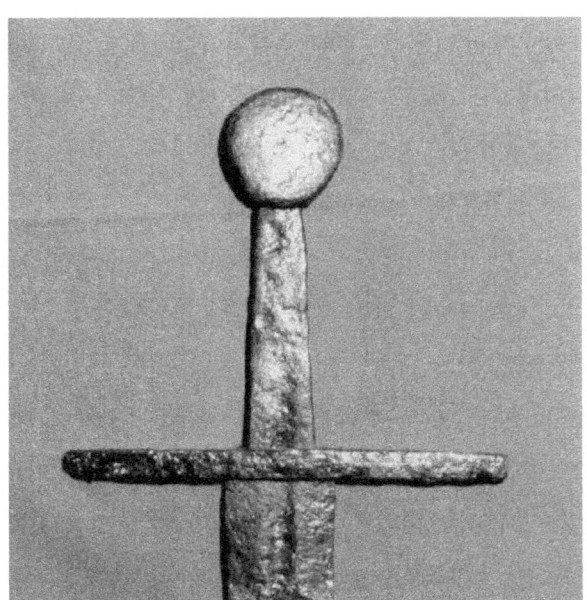

The age of St. Galgano's sword is evident in this photo.
(Photo courtesy Dr. Luigi Garlaschelli)

However, what about Arthur's famous sword, Excalibur? One theory is that Excalibur actually existed as it was reported in the fable. According to Arthurian scholar Geoffrey Ashe, Arthur was supposedly buried at Glastonbury Abbey, which burned down in 1184. In 1190 workers found a slab of stone seven feet deep in the earth and a lead cross inscribed HICIACET SEPULTUS INCLITUS REX ARTURIUS IN INSULA AVALONIA, or "Here lies buried the renowned King Arthur in the Isle of Avalon."

Nine feet further in the earth the workers "unearthed a huge coffin made of a hallowed oak log...Inside was the skeleton of a tall man, the skull damaged, and also some slighter bones with a scrap of yellow hair, presumably the remains of Arthur's queen." [83]

The bones were collected and put with the rest of the abbey's treasures. In 1191, Ashe tells us, Richard I, on his way to the Third Crusade, presented what was said to be Arthur's Excalibur, also found in the grave, to Tancred of Sicily.

Other stories abound, however to indicate that this was not the final disposal of the sword.

According to Adrian Gilbert, the real Excalibur may have been given to King Athelstan of Wessex, the grandson of King Alfred the Great, in the 10th century. After Cromwell gained

---

[83] Ashe, Geoffrey. *The Quest for Arthur's Britain.* New York: Frederick A. Praeger, Publishers 1968, 10.

power in England, the sword disappeared with other crown jewels in 1649. Gilbert believes that Puritans obtained the sword and it wound up in America.

Supposedly, the blade is inscribed and a translation made reads, "The duty of the host is to him who holds the sword." [84] Unfortunately, the discoverers of the sword have chosen not to reveal its current whereabouts or any details concerning how the sword was found.

Although it is popularly believed that Excalibur was the "sword in the stone" of the Arthurian legend, in reality another sword belongs to that part of the legend. Excalibur was given to Arthur by the Lady of the Lake and Merlin who told Arthur "the scabbard was worth ten of the sword for while Arthur carried the scabbard he would never lose blood, no matter how sorely wounded he might be."[85] After Arthur's death, Excalibur was returned to the Lade of the Lake.

Other legendary swords include Durendal, the sword of Roland, which once belonged to Hector of Troy. According to myth, Durendal contained four holy relics in its pommel, a tooth of St. Peter, blood of St. Basil, hair of St. Denis, and a piece of cloth from the clothing of the Virgin Mary.

---

[84] Gilbert, Adrian, et al. *The Holy Kingdom: The Quest for the Real King Arthur.* London: Bantam/Transworld Publishers Ltd. 1998, 288.
[85] Dixon-Kennedy, Mike. *Arthurian Myth & Legend.* London: Blandford 1995, 102.

The supposed site of Arthur's grave, Glastonbury Abbey.
(Photo by Gary R. Varner)

Roland's sword, Durandal, stuck in the walls of Rocamadour, France.

According to the Song of Roland, Roland attempts to destroy the sword to prevent the invading Saracens from capturing it. However, the sword is indestructible so Roland throws the blade into a poisoned stream. Other stories tell the sword's fate differently. "Roland, after trying in vain to shatter his great sword, Durendal, on the rocks, places it and (his) horn beneath him, his face turned toward the Saracen army...Roland dies, and angels from heaven bear his soul aloft." [86]

---

[86] Cavendish, Richard. ed. *Legends of the World.*. New York: Barnes & Noble Books 1994, 219.

Local folklore says that this legendary sword continues to exist and is preserved, stuck in a wall at Rocamadour, France. Rocamadour was also allegedly a place of sanctuary for Mary after the crucifixion of Jesus.

Another sword associated with Roland and the Durendal is Almace. According to Norse legend there were three swords forged by the underworld smithy Wayland, these were Curtana, Almace and Durendal. These swords were presented to Charlemagne to secure the release of a Norse prisoner. According to the story, Charlemagne tested each sword to determine the strength and sharpness. The Curtana penetrated a steel mound "a hands breadth" but damaged, Almace penetrated the steel by a hands breadth without damage and Durendal penetrated "half the length of a man's foot." Curtana was given to Ogier the Dane, Almace to Bishop Turpin, and Durendal (originally kept by Charlemagne) was eventually given to Roland after Charlemagne was instructed to do so in a dream.

Turpin, the archbishop of Reims, was one of the last three Franks to die at the Battle of Roncevaux Pass, Roland and Gualter de Hum were the other two. The Battle of Roncevaux Pass occurred in 778 CE when the Moors surprised Charlemagne's rear guard, led by Roland, and annihilated them.

Charlemagne eventually defeated the Moors and, in the process, reclaimed Spain as a Christian land.

It is interesting that the Song of Roland as well as the tales of King Arthur were written around the time of St. Galgano.

It is likely that the sword was associated with magic and supernatural powers simply due to being forged from metal ore. This process in itself was considered magical as evidenced with

the myths concerning Wayland and the other underworld smiths. Taking raw ore from the ground and transforming it into object of deadly beauty was a wondrous fete.

Other mythic swords include the magic sword of the Norse god Frey that could strike out on its own, and the enchanted sword, Tyrfing, forged by dwarves for Svafrlami, king of Gardariki, grandson of the god Odin that supposedly would never miss a stroke, never rust and would cut through iron and stone as easily as cutting through butter.

Unfortunately, for Svafrlami, the dwarves were evil and cursed the blade so that each time the sword was drawn from its scabbard a man would be killed. Eventually the sword killed Svafrlami as well as the Swedish hero Hjalmar.

Norse blades were often magic in myth. Beowulf had Hrunting, which was said to never fail although it did fail the hero when he descended to the bottom of a lake to combat the evil mother of Grendel. Luckily, Beowulf was able to find another supernatural sword that had belonged to the Giants with which he decapitated her. The creature's poisonous blood, however, melted the Giant's sword like wax.

The 12th and 13th centuries appear to have been a time for great sagas to be told and greater swords to be forged. Snorri Sturluson, an Icelandic historian and poet, wrote the Prose Edda in 1220 CE. The wondrous sword Gram (meaning "wrath" or "angry") is part of that saga. According to Sturluson, Gram was made for the Norse hero Sigurd by the king's craftsman, Regin.[87] The sword was so sharp "that when Sigurd put it down in running water, it cut in two a tuft of wool that drifted with the current against the sword's edge. Next Sigurd split Regin's anvil down to its base with the sword."[88]

---

[87] Other legends say that the sword was made by Wayland, the smith of Celtic importance.
[88] Sturluson, Snorri. *Edda*. Trans. By Anthony Faulkes. London: Everyman Books 1987, 101.

"Sigmund's Sword" (1889) by Johannes Gehrts.

Norse legends say that Odin, appearing as a beggar at a feast, buried Gram into a massive oak with one stroke, saying "Let him of this company who can pull it out, bear it, and none shall say he bore a better blade." Like the legendary Excalibur, "Many tried to possess himself of the sword, but none could draw it from the oak, till Sigmund, the bravest of Volsung's sons, laid his hand upon its hilt. At his touch, it freed itself from the mighty oak..."[89]

Sigurd, Sigmund's son, has many adventures with his sword including cutting the chain mail from a Valkyrie and slaying a dragon. Like many mythic heroes' Sigurd is killed but as he lay

---

[89] Grant, James. *The Mysteries of all Nations*. Leith: Reid & Son 1880, 91.

dying, he threw Gram at his assailant "so that it severed the man in two in the middle." [90]

Legendary swords seem to have the same ability to cut through steel, iron, and rock. Siegurd's sword cut through Regin's anvil, Arthur's sword was embedded in a stone, as is Galgano's. The Celtic hero Fin had a sword called "the son of Luin" which could "cut through six feet of whatever substance was struck by it, and an inch beyond." [91]

Another Norse saga, Gripssonar, tells of Mistelteinn, a sword taken from the "undead" witch-king Prainn. Mistelteinn magically could never go blunt for its user.

Other Medieval swords from European history include Szczerbiec (meaning, "notched"). This sword is the last surviving piece of the Polish crown jewels and was used in every Polish coronation from Wladyslaw Lokietek (also known as Wladyslaw the Short, or Elbow-high, see illustration next page) from January 20, 1320 until Poland was partitioned in 1792. Originally, the sword was said to have been used by Boleslaus the Brave and was notched when he struck the Golden Gate of Kiev in 1018.

---

[90] Ibid., 103.
[91] Campbell, John Gregory. *The Gaelic Otherworld*. Edinburgh: Birlinn 2005, 49.

The sword Szczerbiec had a tumultuous history, captured by the Prussians in 1796 and taken to Berlin and then to Russia. It was given back to Poland in 1928 by Russia.

When World War II broke out in 1939 it was taken from Poland to France for safekeeping and then, in 1940, moved to Canada.

< Wladyslaw the Short

Finally, in 1959, the sword was returned to Poland and is now kept at the Wawel Royal Castle in Krakow.

The Orient, long recognized as a leader in sword production and for its cult of the sword, which may have resulted in the concept of Chivalry in Europe has its own mythic lore concerning the sword. Perhaps the most legendary sword of Japan is Kusanagi-no-tsurugi, or the "Sword of Gathering Clouds of Heaven." This sword is as important to Japan's legendary history as Excalibur is to Britain.

The sword in Japanese culture is a symbol of enlightenment. In both Buddhist and Shinto traditions, the sword has a spiritual essence and it was not uncommon for the blades to be engraved with the forms of various deities.

According to Japanese lore, Kusanagi was believed to have magical powers; it was first given to the grandson of the sun goddess. The grandson was about to become an Emperor and this mythological weapon was a link of the divine world to that of the earth.

Satsuma samurai photographed 1860 by Felice Beato

The swords origin is found in myth. A Japanese god by the name of Susano-O-No-Mikoto came upon a man who told him that his family was being harassed by an eight-headed dragon that had already eaten seven of the man's eight daughters. Susano, in exchange for the hand of the man's one remaining daughter in marriage, sat eight vats of rice wine on platforms behind a fence with eight gates. The dragon scented the wine and stuck each of its heads into each gate. Susano decapitated each head and then struck off each of the dragon's eight tails. In one tale, he found a great sword, which he named Ame Murakumo-No-Tsurugi, or "Sword of Gathering Clouds."[92]

Centuries later, the sword was given to Yamato-Dake, a great warrior. "Kusanagi" means "grasscutter," getting its name from Yamato-Dake's mythic story. A Japanese hero, Yamato-Dake, was given the sword by his aunt so that he could protect himself. On one journey, he was pursued by a local warlord who shot flaming arrows into the grass around Yamato to trap him. The hero began to cut the grass with his sword when he noticed that the direction he cut resulted in the fire going in that direction as well—he had discovered that the sword had magical powers to control the wind and fire. Yamato-Dake made the fire turn back on the warlord, eventually defeating him.

After this, the history of the sword gets a bit muddied. According to an ancient book called the *Nishonshoki*, the sword had been taken to the imperial palace where it was removed in 688 CE to the Arsuta Shrine. The reason it had been removed from the palace is that it had been blamed for causing the Emperor Temmu to become ill.

---

[92] The true meaning of Kusanagi is most likely different. In ancient Japanese *kusa* meant sword and *nagi* meant snake, so the true name was probably Sword of the Snake.

Reportedly, the sword remains in the Arsuta Shrine to this day although it has never been displayed. A Shinto priest who claimed to have seen the sword supposedly died from the swords curse. Other legends say that the sword was lost at sea after the Imperial Navy was defeated in the Battle of Dan-no-ura in 1185 CE.

Other legends say that the sword was stolen during the reign of the tenth emperor from the palace or stolen during the 6th century by a Chinese monk. The latter legend states that the monk's ship sank and the sword was washed up on the Isle of Ise where Shinto priests recovered it. Regardless of its whereabouts, Kusanagi is still considered a sacred sword of Japan.

A modern day photo of Arsuta Shrine, perhaps the home of the sacred Kusanagi sword.

The Middle East has its share of mythic swords as well, from El Cid's Tizona to Shamshir-e Zomorrodnegar and Zulfiqar. Our first sword is that of Shamshir-e Zomorrodnegar, the "emerald studded sword" of Persia (contemporary Iran). In the legend of Amir Arsalan, a horned demon called Fulad-zereh existed. The demon's witch-mother charmed her demon son to make him invulnerable to any weapon except Shamshir-e Zomorrodnegar.

To wear the sword was a charm against magic and any wound suffered from it could only be treated by a magic potion made from various ingredients, including the brains of Fulad-zereh. According to myth, this sword originally belonged to King Solomon.

From Solomon we next move on to the prophet Muhammad and his sword, Zulfiqar. Zulfiqar was, of course, a scimitar. In lore this sword was actually used by both Muhammad and his son-in-law, Ali and it is Ali who is most often spoken of in association with the sword.

Islamic tradition says that Ali used the sword to strike an opponent and the blade split the man and his horse in two. The legends say that the blade would have split the earth down the middle as well except the Archangel Gabriel intervened. The opponent was Marhab, the Jewish leader at the fort of Khaybar.

Since that time, Zulfiqar has been used as a symbol for several Islam nations and the Shiá Muslims chant "La fatà illa

Ali, la saif illa Zulfiqar" meaning "there is no hero except Ali, there is no sword except Zulfiqar." This saying used to be inscribed on all new weapons. The word Zulfiqar is thought to mean "cleaver of the spine" or "double-edged one" and it has been interpreted to mean the clear difference between right and wrong or the one who makes such a distinction.

Burton has a somewhat different history of this sword. Calling it the "Lord of Cleaving," Burton says that the sword was given to Mohammed by the Archangel Gabriel. It was then given to Ali "who cleft with it the skull of Marhab, the giant Jew warrior of Khaybar Fort." [93]

The green and white flag of Saudi Arabia, prominently displaying Muhammad's sword, Zulfiqar.

---

[93] Burton, Richard F. *The Book of the Sword.* New York: Dover Publications, Inc.1987, 141

His translation of the Moslem saying is somewhat crude as well: "there is no sword to be compared, for doing damage to the foe, with Zú'l-Fikár, and no valiant youth but Ali." [94]

Our final historic and mythic sword is Tizona, the sword of El Cid. Tizona was used by El Cid to fight the Moors in Spain and remains one of Spain's sacred relics and is now in the Musem del Ejército (Military Museum) in Madrid. Part of its strength undoubtedly is due to it being at least partially forged of Damascus steel.

There are two inscriptions on the blade, one reads: "I am 'La Tizona,' made in the year 1040" and the other "Hail Mary, full of grace. The Lord is with you." Even though El Cid is a major Catholic hero, his allegiance was not so definite. He fought against the Moors, it is true, but he also fought for the Moors against the Christians. He is one of the few warriors who are revered by both faiths.

Recently the actual history of the sword in the Military Museum has come under scrutiny. It was purchased by the Spanish regions of Castile and Leon recently for two million dollars so that it could be displayed at the tomb of El Cid in the cathedral of Burgos. However, after its purchase the Culture Ministry announced that El Cid never held this particular sword in his hand. In fact, the Culture Ministry related that the sword

---

[94] Ibid.

had been forged in the 14th or 15th centuries, long after the hero's death.

Statue of El Cid, Burgos, Spain.

While the sword sold for $2,000,000 the true value, says the Culture Ministry, is somewhere around $250,000. Castile and Leon believe that the Culture Ministry is simply jealous due to losing custody of the relic, stressing that the sword is authentic. The "launching" of the sword will take place on the 800th anniversary of El Cid at the Burgos Cathedral. [95]

Magical Inscriptions-Magical Blades

As noted, many warriors sought a mystical quality to add to their weapon to ensure success in battle and ultimately to ensure their very survival. Many of these efforts included added signs or numbers etched into the blade. Many of these have been identified as astrological symbols, others have cabbalistic meanings known only to the owner and the sorcerer who sold him the spell.

Dating the origin of magically incised blades is not possible but we do know that the Celts of the La Tène culture imbued their weapons with supernatural powers through this technique. Ancient blades were also decorated with important cultural images such as the engraving of a Viking war ship dating to the middle of the second millennium BC found on a sword from Kalundborg, Denmark.

By the 15th century the engraving of blades was still common, at least among the aristocracy. The images were not so much of a magical nature designed for the individual but were of classical scenes from mythology which, symbolically, did impart some of

---

[95] Tarvainen, Sinikka. "Row erupts in Spain over legendary knight El Cid's sword" June 10, 2007, Monsters and Critics.com

the older supernatural feeling. Over time, engraved blades became more common among hunting swords rather than military weapons. However, the magical symbolism was still important to ensure the success of the hunt and protection to the hunter. Many of these magical signs originated on German hunting swords and by the 18th century, the practice was fairly universal.

Chapter Three
Sword Lore

Swords have a certain place in our folklore. As Cooper noted, the sword "possesses supernatural powers, either on the earth, under earth, or under the waters, and is associated with giants and supernatural beings...it is also wielded by the cosmic or solar Hero, conqueror of dragons and demonic powers." [96] Strangely enough, swords are also part of the lore of folk medicine. During the 1890's toothaches were said to be cured by rusty swords—in what manner we may never know. An account from Sweden in the 1920's reported the following folk treatment:

"The power of 'Harmful iron' is commonly known all around the country. By this one means iron, e.g. knives, axes, swords and bayonets that have been used to commit murder. If such iron is used to stroke a sick limb, e.g. one that is swollen or has a tumor, it will get again right away."[97]

Another interesting use for the sword was recorded among German and East European Jews. Theodor Gaster wrote, "a bronze or steel sword was hung over the head of women in childbirth... (and) Childbed scenes in Kirchner's Jüdisches

---

[96] Cooper, J.C. *An Illustrated Encyclopaedia of Traditional Symbols.* London: Thames and Hudson 1978, 167.
[97] Storaker, Joh. Th. "Naturrigerne i den Norske Folketro." Norsk Folkeminnelag No. 18, Oslo 1928, 29.

Ceremoniel (1726) shows sword prominently displayed beside the bed." [98] It is doubtful that a woman in labor was very appreciative to have a sword hanging over her head while in childbirth although it may have motivated her to deliver the child as soon as she could!

Grant wrote, "If the snaffle of a bridle be made of a sword that has killed a man, the rider may with ease control a horse, however wild the animal may be; and if a sword that has been used in beheading a person be dipped in wine, it will impart a medicinal virtue to the liquor."[99]

In some cultures, swords were used as strong measures against demons. The Ainu, an indigenous people of Japan, believe that a demon they call Sarak Kamui, is responsible for accidents. According to folklorist John Batchelor, "When the Ainu arrive at the scene of an accident, they howl and strike the spot with swords to drive away this evil demon." [100] Magicians in ancient China are also pictured driving demons away with swords.

In ancient Cambodia two kings ruled. One was the King of Fire and the other the King of Water. The more powerful of the two, the King of Fire, officiated at marriages, festivals and

---

[98] Gaster, Theordor H. *The Holy and the Profane*. New York: William Sloane Associates 1955, 10.
[99] Grant, James. *The Mysteries of all Nations*. Leith: Reid & Son 1880
[100] Batchelor, John. "Items of Ainu Folk-Lore" in *Journal of American Folklore*, No. 7 (1894), 20.

sacrifices. The sacrifices were to the *Yan* — a powerful spirit. The King of Fire's supernatural abilities and powers were never disputed.

Traditionally the King descended along family lines. The family possessed the sacred talismans that were used in the festivals and rituals that the King of Fire presided over. These talismans were the *Cui*, the still green fruit of a vine that had been gathered in ancient times from the last deluge, a rattan bat that bore flowers that never faded, and a sword that actually contained the Yan, or spirit, that not only protected the sword but also used it to work miracles. [101]

According to Frazer, the yan, or spirit "is said to be that of a slave, whose blood chanced to fall upon the blade while it was being forged, and who died a voluntary death to expiate his involuntary offence (of bleeding on the blade). [102]

The powers of the sword were so potent hat special protection had to be provided which included sacrifices of buffaloes, pigs, fowls and ducks. In addition, it was wrapped in cotton and silk.

Frazer noted that should the Fire King "draws the magic sword a few inches from its sheath, the sun is hidden and men

---

[101] Frazer, Sir James. *The Golden Bough: A study in magic and religion.* Hertfordshire: Wordsworth Editions Ltd., 1993, 108.
[102] Ibid.

and beasts fall into a profound sleep; were he to draw it quite out of the scabbard, the world would come to an end." [103]

Another legendary sword is Sköfnung, the sword of the Viking Hrolf Kraki. According to historian R. Ewart Oakeshott, Sköfnung "was the best of all swords which have been carried in the northern lands."[104] The sword was said to "utter a loud cry whenever it saw wounds." Part of its magic lay in a charm called the "life stone" that enabled any wound caused by the sword to be healed only if the life stone was rubbed in the wound. Legends of these "life stones" were common between 200 and 600 CE and archaeologists believe that large, perforated beads, made of stone, glass, pottery or meerschaum normally found on battle swords affixed near the hilt were these "life stones." "The frequency with which these things turn up," wrote Oakeshott, "and the constant position of all of them near the sword hilt, makes it obvious that they were fixed, probably by a lace or a thong, either to the hilt itself in the manner of the sword knot, or to the top of the scabbard." [105]

The charm was protected by the sword's owner to ensure that it would be effective if needed. The full sun could not shine on the swords pommel, nor could the sword be drawn when

---

[103] Ibid., 109.
[104] Oakeshott, R. Ewart. *The Archaeology of Weapons*. Mineola: Dover Publications, Inc. 1996, 103.
[105] Ibid., 104.

women were near or in sight of anyone else. To fail in any of this would prohibit the blade from being withdrawn from its scabbard, which would result in the death of its user in times of battle.

The use of the sword as a symbol is an ancient one. A sword is still used for the coronation of the queen of England and to open Parliament—as such it is a symbol of royalty and justice.

The following bits of lore illustrate the folk nature of the sword in various cultures and times.

The Good Swerd of Winfarthyng

The "Good Swerd of Winfarthyng" was a real weapon with a past so old that its origin and identity was long forgotten by the time Thomas Becon wrote of it in 1563. The sword, kept in a parish church in the small village of Winfarthing in Norfolk, "was counted so precious a Relique, and of so great Virtue," Becon wrote, "that there was a solemne Pilgrimage used to unto it, wyth large Giftes and Offringes, with Vow markings, Crouchinges, & Kissinges: This Swerd was visited far and near, for many & sundry Purposes, but specially for thinges that were lost, and for horses that were eyther stolen or else rune astray, it helped also unto the Shortening of a married Mans Life, if that the Wyfe which was weary of her Husband, would set a Candle before the Swerd every Sunday excepted, for then all was vain, whatsoever was done before." [106]

Unfortunately, the "Good Swerd" was one of the objects of devotion, which was destroyed in the Reformation.

Talking Swords

According to 19th century folklorist James Bonwick, Irish swords would turn against their owner and speak their curses if "false trophies" were taken in battle. At the time, the tongues of enemies were taken as trophies. An ancient manuscript titled *Leb na huidre* recorded:

"And it is thus they ought to do that, and their swords on their thighs when they used to make the trophy, for their swords used to turn against them when they made a false trophy—for demons used to speak to them in their arms." [107]

Bonwick quotes an Irish source when he wrote, "So do the Irish to this day, when they go to battle, say certain prayers or charms to their swords, making a cross therewith upon the earth, and thrusting the points of their blades into the ground,

---

[106] Becon, Thomas. *Reliques of Rome*, 1563.
[107] Bonwick, James. *Irish Druids and Old Irish Religions.* New York: Barnes & Noble, Inc. 1986, 136.

thinking thereby to have a better success in fight. Also they commonly to swear by their swords."[108]

Lady Gregory tells us "It was in this battle Ogma found Orna, the sword of Tethra, a king of the Fomor, and he took it from its sheath and cleaned it. And when the sword was taken out of the sheath, it told all the deeds that had been done by it, for there used to be that power in swords." [109]

Other Blades of Mythology & Folklore

We have already discussed many magical and heroic swords belonging to King Arthur, Mohammad, El Cid and others but we would be remiss to leave out some other swords with as colorful pasts as the others.

One of these is the Sword of Strange Hangings. According to Dixon-Kennedy, the Sword of Strange Hangings "belonged to the biblical King David of Israel. His son, Solomon, placed it aboard his ship, where it hung in hempen hangings made by Solomon's wife. This sword later appeared in the Arthurian legends, and had the hempen hangings replaced by some made from the hair of Perceval's sister. [110]

Celtic lore is full of magical swords used by heroic figures. At times, the individual who used the magical swords was not

---

[108] Ibid., 137.
[109] Gregory, Lady. *Gods and Fighting Men.* London: J. Murray 1905
[110] Dixon-Kennedy, Mike. *Arthurian Myth & Legend.* London: Blandford 1995, 262.

as extraordinary as simply being in the right place at the right time. One of these stories involved a ship sailing from Greenock in Scotland. According to the story, three witches were set on destroying the ship unless "three rolling waves…were cut with a sword." "At the time said," according to legend, "the apprentice was allowed to command the vessel, and standing in the bow with a drawn sword, cleft the waves and defeated the witches."[111]

Distinct "male" and "female" swords are mentioned in Chinese lore, supposedly forged from the kidneys of a mythic rabbit said to live in the Kuenlun Mountains. This mythic rabbit reportedly ate metal. [112]

Folklore continues to exist in association with bladed weapons. During World War II, Levine & Weland wrote, Allied Gurkha troops were noted to always prick their finger when returning their knives to their sheath. "This was done because of a local tradition, which stated that a weapon could not return to its sheath by a living Gurkha, without tasting blood!" [113]

---

[111] Campbell, John Gregory. *The Gaelic Otherworld.* Edinburgh: Birlinn 2005, 183.
[112] Biedermann, Hans. *Dictionary of Symbolism.* New York: Meridian 1994, 335.
[113] Levine, Bernard and Gerald Weland. *Knives, Swords, Daggers.* New York: Barnes & Noble Books 2004, 204.

The Sword of Tyr

The Norsemen lived, died and worshipped with the sword. It would only seem logical that they would have a patron god of the sword as well. Tyr was that god. Each sword owned and made by the Norsemen had a rune or other symbol of Tyr engraved on its blade—an insurance policy for victory.

According to Gale Owen, "The runic symbol ↑ represented the name of Tiw (Tyr) and was traditionally carved on weapons to ensure victory. The Icelandic poem *Sigrdriformâl* provides interesting, if late, evidence of this practice (the text is thirteenth century). A Valkyrie instructs a hero about different kinds of runes. She tells him 'victory runes' should be carved on the hilt of a sword, on the ridge along the blade,...and that the name of the god 'Ty' should be carved twice." [114]

She further notes that the runic symbol ↑, "which represented the name of the god Tir, were prehistoric devices, religious or magical symbols in use from ancient times." [115] Each rune also had a phonetic value and, in this case, the ↑ not only represented the name of the god but also the sound *t*. It is interesting that two complete runic alphabets have been discovered over the years, one of them on a manuscript located

---

[114] Owen, Gale R. *Rites and Religions of the Anglo-Saxons*. Dorset Press 1985, 28-29.
[115] Ibid, 52.

in Vienna, and the other engraved on a sword that was found in the Thames—placed there as a votive offering.

The arrow symbol has been found on Anglo-Saxon sword pommels and spears and is one of the most common symbols found engraved on English cremation urns. Tyr is believed to be synonymous with the Saxon sword-god, Saxnet who, like Odin and Thor, was worshipped widely until the 8th and 9th centuries.

Tyr was not only the god of war and of the sword; he was a sky-god to the Norsemen and was either the son of Odin or of the giant Hymir. Tyr was believed to have the ability to "decide which side would prevail in combat." [116]Because of this, he was often invoked prior to battle.

Tyr was also a god of order. As Davidson noted, "Tyr stood for rule by law." [117]

A large scimitar was used as a symbol of Ares, the Greek God of War, by the ancient Scythians. Herodotus wrote:

"To the other gods they sacrifice thus and these kinds of beasts, but to Ares as follows:--In each district of the several tribal territories they have a temple of Ares set up in this way:-- bundles of brushwood are heaped up for about 1800 feet square, but less in height; and on top a level square is made...Upon this pile of which I speak each people has an ancient scimitar set up,

---

[116] Baker, Alan. *The Viking*. Hoboken: John Wiley & Sons, Inc. 2004, 87.
[117] Davidson, Hilda Ellis. *The Lost Beliefs of Northern Europe*. New York: Barnes & Noble, Inc. 1993, 154.

and this offering represents Ares. To this scimitar they bring yearly offerings of cattle and of horses; and they have the following sacrifice in addition, beyond what they make to the other gods. They sacrifice one man in every hundred of all the enemies whom they take captive in war…They first pour wine over their heads, and after that they cut the throats of the men, so that the blood runs into a bowl; and then they carry this up to the top of the pile of brushwood and pour the blood over the sword…"[118]

According to legend, Tyr's sword disappeared until it was discovered by the Duke of Alva, who soon after retrieving the sword, won a military victory at Mühlberg in 1547. According to Helene Guerber, "The Franks were won't to celebrate yearly martial games in honor of the sword; but it is said that when the heathen gods were renounced in favor of Christianity, the priests transferred many of their attributes to the saints, and that the sword became the property of the Archangel St. Michael, who has wielded it ever since." [119]

---

[118] Herodotus. *The Histories.* Trans. by G.C. Macaulay. New York: Barnes & Noble Classics, 215-216.
[119] Guerber, Helene A. *Myths of the Norsemen.* New York: Barnes & Noble 2006, 96.

Chapter Four
The Sword Dance

The sword dance is an ancient dance, actually more ritual than dance and it survives today in Great Britain and in other European countries where survivals of supposed pagan traditions continue to draw crowds.

Such a dance was performed by the Norsemen in honor of their God of War, Tyr, son of Odin. According to historian Helene A. Guerber, the Norse, "venerating the god as they did, were wont to worship him under the emblem of the sword…and in his honor held great sword dances…" [120]

Guerber describes the dance as follows:

"Sometimes the participants forming two long lines, crossed their swords, point upward, and challenged the boldest among their number to take a flying leap over them. At other times the warriors joined their sword points closely together in the shape of a rose or wheel, and when this figure was complete invited their chief to stand on the naval thus formed of flat, shining steel blades, and then they bore him upon it through the camp in triumph." [121]

---

[120] Guerber, Helene A. *Myths of the Norsemen*. New York: Barnes & Noble 2006, 92.
[121] Ibid.

Burton noted, "Athenaeus speaks of the Thracian dance in arms, 'men jumping up very high with light springs, and using swords.' At last one of them strikes another, so that it seemed to everyone that the man was wounded.'

He continues, quoting an Italian writer by the name of Edmondo de Amicis who wrote of a dance he observed in Tangier:

"'There were three swordsmen, and they used the stick in pairs. It is impossible to do justice to the extravagance and buffoonery of that *school:* I call it so because we saw the same style in the other cities of Morocco. There were all the movements of the rope-dance, high leaps without object, contusions, leg-actions, and blows, announced a whole minute before by an immense sweep of the arm. Everything was done with a holy phlegm which would have allowed one of our experts to have distributed, amongst all four, a volley of blows without the least risk of receiving one.'" [122]

Referred to as "linked" or "hilt and point" dances in England, the participants would hold on to the hilt of their sword with one hand and the point of their neighbor's sword, creating a linked circle. Their were two dances in England that made up the sword dance, one called the Longsword which was accomplished with a basic walking step, and the other called the

---

[122] Burton, Richard F. *The Book of the Sword.* New York: Dover Publications, Inc. 1987, 163.

"Rapper Dance" which used a shorter sword. As Simpson and Round wrote, "…Rapper dancers execute a special step which beats a staccato rhythm on the floor…their dance is much tighter and apparently faster." [123]

The origins of the sword dance appear to date to the 14th century and scant references were made to it between 1604 and the 18th century. Many scholars who attempt to discredit ancient origins for ritual, folklore and dance to pre-Christian times believe that the sword dance is no more than 200 years old and that attempts to link it to ancient pagan rituals have not been overly successful. However, others claim that the sword dance was described by Plato, obviously taking place much further back in time. L. W. Yaggy and T. L. Haines wrote in their book, *Museum of Antiquity*, "Amongst the pictures of female jugglers in all kinds of impossible postures, can be seen a girl performing the dangerous sword-dance, described by Plato. It consists in her turning somersaults forwards and backwards across the points of three swords stuck in the ground…"[124]

Sword dances were common around the world and were popular in the Low Countries, across central Europe, Sweden, the Iberian Peninsula, Asia and Africa. While the dance was

---

[123] Simpson, Jacqueline and Steve Roud. *Oxford Dictionary of English Folklore.* Oxford: Oxford University Press 2000, 350.
[124] Yaggy, L. W. and T. L. Haines. *Museum of Antiquity.* MadisonL J. B. Furman & Co. 1884

popular during the 14th century in Europe and the Middle East, it was also practiced in 7th century Korea.

A cave painting dating between 57 BC to 668 BC depicts a female warrior with sword in hand in a dance pose. Called the *Geom-mu,* the dance is thought to have originated in its present form during the Three Kingdoms of Korea era around 66 CE.

"The documentary records strongly support the view that sword dancing developed as a performance style in urban festivals of the Late Middle Ages," writes Steven Corrsin, "an era in which carrying swords was a mark of honor and respect..." [125]

Another sword dance originating in Albania, called the Pyrrhic dance, was introduced into ancient Rome by Caesar who introduced it into the public games.

In Europe, the dance slowly died out as warfare engulfed the continent in the 16th century and Church prohibitions against popular festivals became more stringent. It can still be found in many areas of the world as a folk-dance.

---

[125] Corrsin, Steven D. "Sword Dance" in *Medieval Folklore.* Oxford: Oxford University Press 2002, 401.

Late 19th - early 20th century photo of a Sudanese sword dance

Chapter Five
The Modern Reproduction

Collecting swords and daggers is an extremely popular hobby which can be enjoyed for the craftsmanship exhibited in the item as well as the history. The photos on the following pages are presented to show the potential collector what types of blades are available. With some exception, these are reproductions based on historical weapons.

A horse-headed dagger similar to the highly decorated blades of the Ottoman Empire and India. (Author's collection)

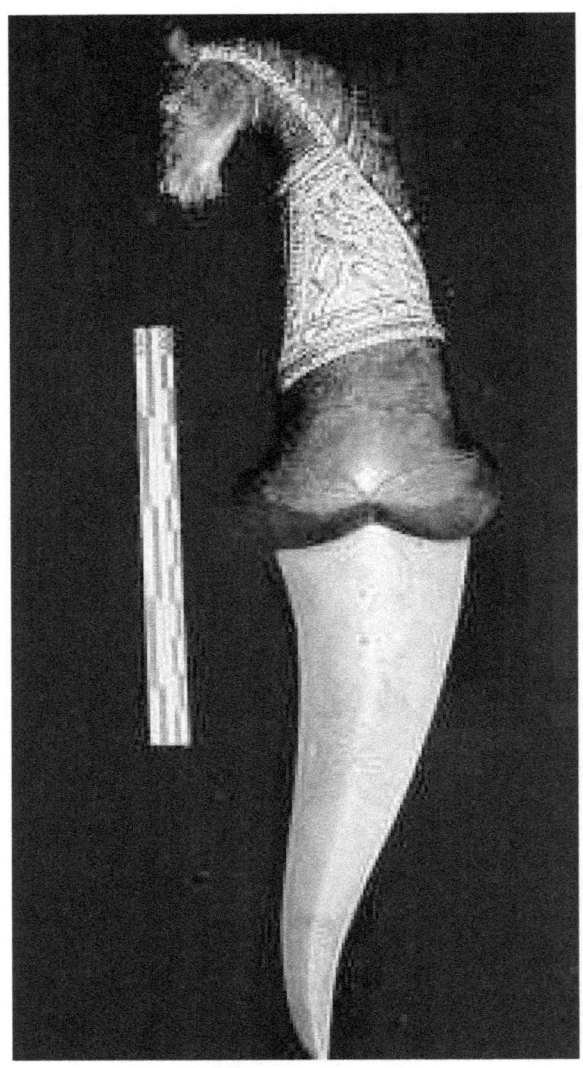

A dagger similar to that shown on the previous page. This one is from India and of the Asaf Jahi period, 150 years ago. The middle part of the hilt is made of jade and the blade from brass. (Photo: The Hindu)

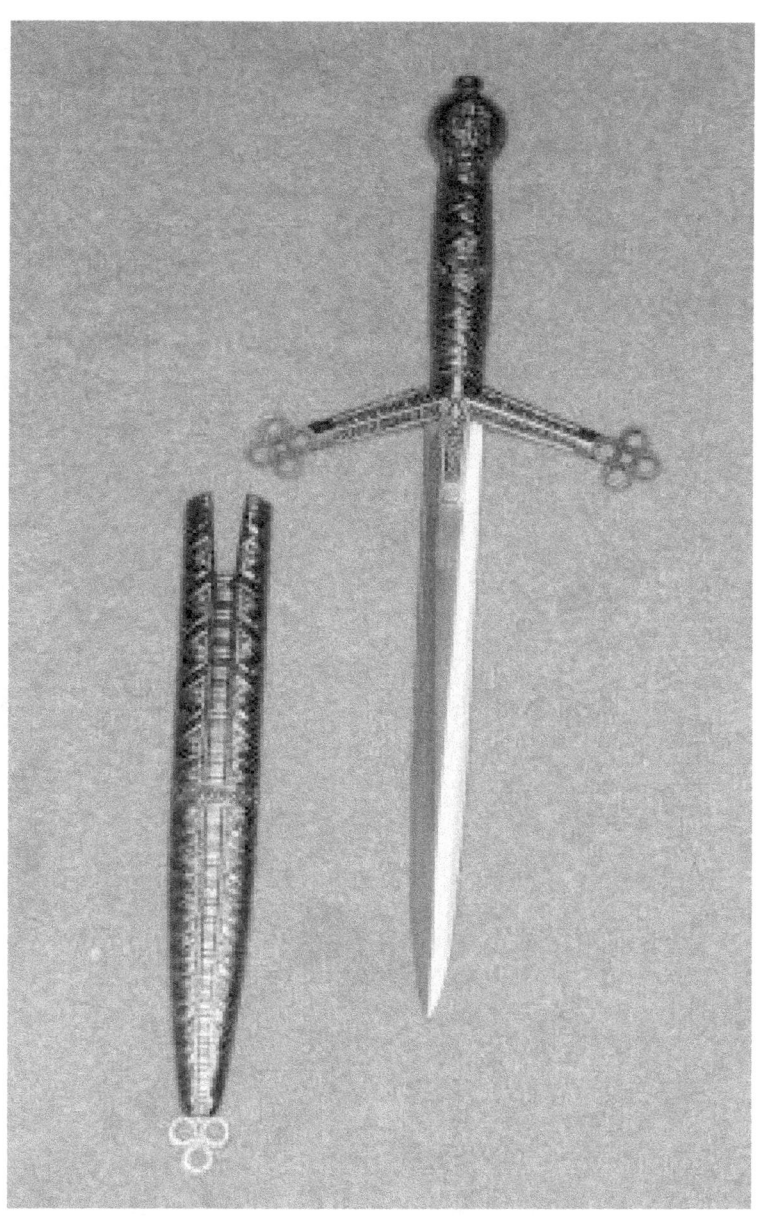

Large dagger styled after a left-handed quillon dagger of the 16th century. (Author's collection)

Contemporary dagger in the medieval style.
(Author's collection)

Dagger with a mythic mermaid figure as the pommel. The highly decorated scabbard is modeled from a Swiss dagger of the late 16th century. Sometimes called the "Holbein dagger", the scabbard was often artistically gilded and engraved in historic or mythic scenes by the leading artists of the day. (Author's collection)

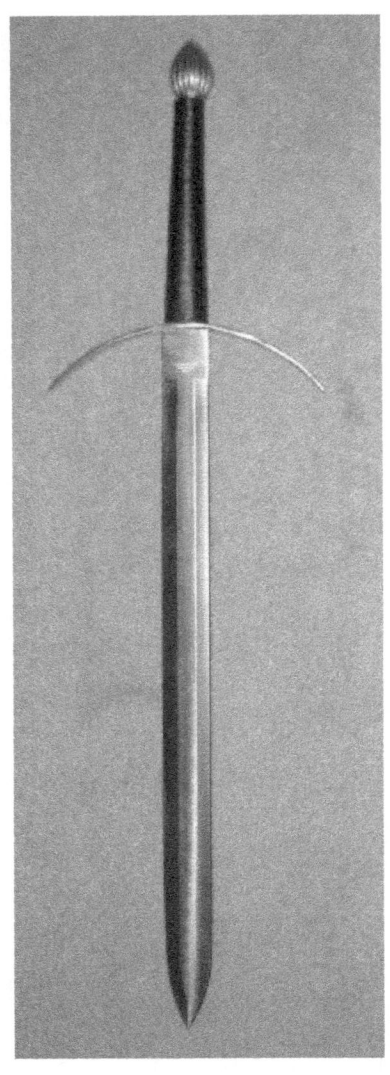

Short sword styled on the 16th century weapon.
(Author's collection)

Highly decorative dagger with engraved blade, pommel and scabbard. (Author's collection)

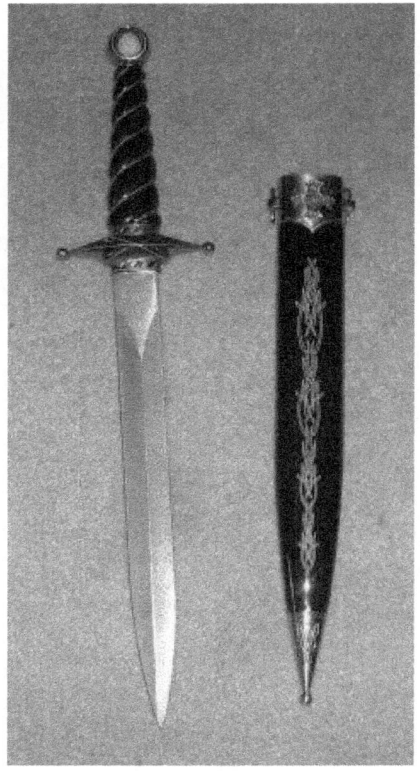

Typical 15th/16th century thrusting blade.

Sword collecting has become the number one hobby in America over the last few years. For the most part this is due to the history of the sword and the sword's association with myth as well as its artistic attributes.

Hayward noted that "the most interesting lesson of...the history of the sword during a period of 300 years is its illustration of the sword designer's determination to produce a work of art. Although considerations of defence were inevitably a determining factor in the design, at no time was the craftsman satisfied with the achievement of functional qualities along." [126]

Many excellent historical reproductions may be purchased for relatively inexpensive amounts. Any person interested in collecting bladed weapons is advised to contact the following vendors:

Collector's Armoury, Ltd. (www.collectorsarmoury.com)

The BudK Catalog (www.budk.com)

BladeEmpire.com

An excellent source for factual and historic information on swords and other ethnographic weapons is the

---

[126] Hayward, J.F. *Swords & Daggers.* London: Victorian and Albert Museum/Her Majesty's Stationery Office 1963, 10.

Ethnographic Arms and Armour Forum which can be found at the following internet address:

http://www.vikingsword.com/vb/index.php?

The collector should be aware that the same item might have a wide variety of prices depending on the vendor so caution is always suggested.

For real weapons, one should search out antique dealers and thrift shops as often as possible. eBay is another good source. The potential buyer is cautioned, however, as modern reproductions are often fraudulently sold at high prices and are listed as authentic items.

About the Author

Gary R. Varner, long a collector of bladed weapons has written several books and articles on folklore, mythology and ancient history including *The Dark Wind: Witches and the Concept of Evil* and *Gargoyles, Grotesques & Green Men: Ancient Symbolism in European and American Architecture*. He is a member of the American Folklore Society and has been included in several editions of *Who's Who in the World* and *Who's Who in America*.

Readers are invited to visit the author's website at www.authorsden.com/garyrvarner.

Bibliography

Ashe, Geoffrey. *The Quest for Arthur's Britain.* New York: Frederick A. Praeger, Publishers 1968

Baker, Alan. *The Viking.* Hoboken: John Wiley & Sons, Inc. 2004

Beer, Robert. *The Handbook of Tibetan Buddhist Symbols.* Boston: Shambhala Publications 2003

Bonwick, James. *Irish Druids and Old Irish Religions.* New York: Barnes & Noble, Inc. 1986

Burton, Richard F. *The Book of the Sword.* New York: Dover Publications, Inc. 1987

Campbell, John Gregory. *The Gaelic Otherworld.* Edinburgh: Birlinn 2005

Corrsin, Steven D. "Sword Dance" in *Medieval Folklore.* Oxford: Oxford University Press 2002

Cunliffe, Barry. *The Ancient Celts.* Oxford: Oxford University Press 1997

Davidson, H.R. Ellis. *Gods and Myths of the Viking Age.* New York: Bell Publishing Company 1964

Davidson, H.R. Ellis. *Myths and Symbols in Pagan Europe: Early Scandinavian and Celtic Religions.* Syracuse: Syracuse University Press 1988

Davidson, Hilda Ellis. *The Lost Beliefs of Northern Europe.* New York: Barnes & Noble, Inc. 1993

Davidson, Hilda Ellis. "Sword" in *Medieval Folklore: A Guide to Myths, Legends, Tales, Beliefs, and Customs*. Oxford: Oxford University Press 2000, pgs 399-401.

Fee, Christopher R. *Gods, Heroes, & Kings: The Battle for Mythic Britain*. Oxford: Oxford University Press 2001

Frazer, Sir J.G. *Adonis: A Study in the History of Oriental Religion*. The Thinker's Library, No. 30. London: Watts & Co. 1932

Frazer, Sir James. *The Golden Bough: A study in magic and religion*. Hertfordshire: Wordsworth Editions Ltd., 1993

Fuller, Richard and Ron Gregory. *Military Swords of Japan 1868-1945*. London: Arms and Armour Press 1986

Garlaschelli, Luigi. "The *Real* Sword in the Stone," in *Skeptical Inquirer*, March/April 2006

Gaster, Theordor H. *The Holy and the Profane*. New York: William Sloane Associates 1955

Gilbert, Adrian, et al. *The Holy Kingdom: The Quest for the Real King Arthur*. London: Bantam/Transworld Publishers Ltd. 1998

Grant, James. *The Mysteries of all Nations*. Leith: Reid & Son 1880

Guerber, Helene A. *Myths of the Norsemen*. New York: Barnes & Noble 2006

Hayward, J.F. *Swords & Daggers*. London: Victoria and Albert Museum/Her Majesty's Stationery Office 1963

Herm, Gerhard. *The Celts*. New York: St, Martin's Press, Inc. 1975

Levine, Bernard & Gerald Weland. *Knives, Swords, Daggers.* New York: Barnes & Noble Books 2004

Merrifield, Ralph. *The Archaeology of Ritual and Magic.* New York: New Amsterdam Books 1987

Norman, Vesey. *The Medieval Soldier.* South Yorkshire: Pen & Sword Books Limited 2006

Oakeshott, R. Ewart. *The Archaeology of Weapons.* Mineola: Dover Publications, Inc. 1996

Owen, Gale R. *Rites and Religions of the Anglo-Saxons.* Dorset Press 1985

Paul, E. Jaiwant. *Arms and Armour: Traditional Weapons of India.* New Delhi: Lustre Press/Roli Books 2004

Peterson, Harold L. *Daggers and Fighting Knives of the Western World.* Minneola: Dover Publications, Inc. 2001

Piggott, Stuart. *Ancient Europe from the beginnings of Agriculture to Classical Antiquity.* Chicago: Aldine Publishing Company 1965
Rawson, P.S. *The Indian Sword.* New York: ARCO Publishing Company, Inc. 1968

Regan, Paula, ed. *Weapon: A Visual History of Arms and Armor.* London: DK Books 2006

Sprague, Martina. *Norse Warfare: The Unconventional Battle Strategies of the Ancient Vikings.* New York: Hippocrene Books, Inc. 2007

Sturluson, Snorri. *Edda.* Trans. By Anthony Faulkes. London: Everyman Books 1987

Tarassuk, Leonid and Claude Blair, ed. *The Complete Encyclopedia of Arms & Weapons.* Crown Publishers, Inc. 1986

Tresidder, Jack. *Symbols and Their Meanings.* New York: Barnes & Noble Books 2006

Wills, Chuck. *Weaponry: An Illustrated History.* New York: Hylas Publishing 2006

Yaggy, L. W. and T. L. Haines. *Museum of Antiquity.* MadisonL J. B. Furman & Co. 1884

Yumoto, John M. *The Samurai Sword: A Handbook.* Rutland: Charles E. Tuttle Company 1958

Zimmer, Heinrich. *Myths and Symbols in Indian Art and Civilization.* Ed by Joseph Campbell. Princeton: Princeton University Press/Bollingen Series VI 1972

Index

A

Ares, 105, 106
Asi, the Sword, 60

B

bayonet, 54, 55, 96
Beowulf, 11, 68, 83
Britain, 17, 27, 62, 64, 66, 86, 107
Bronze, 16, 17, 19, 24, 25, 96
Bronze Age, 13, 62, 63
Buddhism, 60, 61

C

cavalry, 30
Celts, 23- 27, 30, 94
charm, 25, 31, 66, 67, 90, 99, 101
Chinese, 21, 53, 89, 103
copper, 13, 16, 19, 31, 42
Cornwall, 16

D

daggers, 15, 16, 18, 19, 24, 28, 29, 34, 41, 47, 49, 50, 56, 57, 63, 113, 114, 115, 116, 117, 119
Damascus, 21, 22, 92
demon, 61, 70, 90, 96, 97, 101

Denmark, 64, 94
Durendal, 66, 78, 80, 81

E

Egypt, 11, 13, 15, 16, 28, 42, 61
El Cid, 90, 92, 93, 94, 102
England, 16, 34, 63, 68, 78, 100, 108
Excalibur, 66, 73, 77, 78, 84, 86

F

flamberg, 70, 74
France, 80, 81, 86
Frey, 82

G

gladius, 20, 27, 28, 29, 30
Germany, 22

H

Hindu, 11, 44
Hrunting, 83
Hunting swords, 95

I

India, 16, 22, 42, 43, 44, 45, 55, 59, 60, 66, 113, 114

iron, 17, 18, 19, 21, 23, 24, 25, 29, 31, 32, 50, 61, 66, 70, 82, 85, 96
Iron Age, 34, 62

J

Japan, 52, 53, 55, 56, 59, 66, 86, 87, 88, 89, 97

K

kard, 45, 46
keris, 70
khanda, 44, 45
King Arthur, 11, 75, 77, 82, 102
kris, 70, 71, 72, 73
Kusanagi, 86, 87, 88, 89

L

La Téne, 23, 24, 25
long swords, 21, 23, 25, 38, 39, 40

M

Mesopotamia, 16, 17
metalsmiths, 22
Minoans, 16
Mohammed, 91

N

Nazi, 56, 57
Norsemen, 104, 105, 107
North Africa, 43
North America, 16

O

offerings, 23, 32, 52, 63, 64, 105, 106
Orient, 52, 86
Oxfordshire, 68

P

Paleolithic, 13
pattern-weld, 32
People of the Sea, 16
Poland, 85, 86
pugio, 27, 28, 29

R

Roland, 78, 80, 81, 82
Roman, 20, 21, 23, 24, 26, 27, 28, 29, 30, 37, 39, 43
Russia, 16, 86

S

sacrifice, 26, 30, 63, 98, 105, 106
samurai, 52, 53, 54, 56, 87
Saxons, 30, 69, 105
Scandinavia, 15, 31, 32, 64
scimitar, 43, 90, 105, 106
scramasax, 33, 34
Scythians, 105
spatha, 30, 37
St. Galgano, 9, 75, 76, 82
steel, 21, 23, 26, 29, 32, 70, 81, 85, 92, 96, 107
sword dance, 107, 108, 109, 110, 111
Sword of Nuadha, 27

sword of wisdom, 61
symbols, 51, 94, 104, 105
Szczerbiec, 85, 86

T

Thames, 63, 105
tin, 16, 17
Tizona, 90, 92
Tuscany, 73, 75, 76
Tyr, 104, 105, 106, 107
Tyrfing, 82

V

Viking, 10, 30, 31, 32, 33, 34, 40, 63, 65, 94, 99

W

wootz steel, 22

Z

Zulfiqar, 90, 91

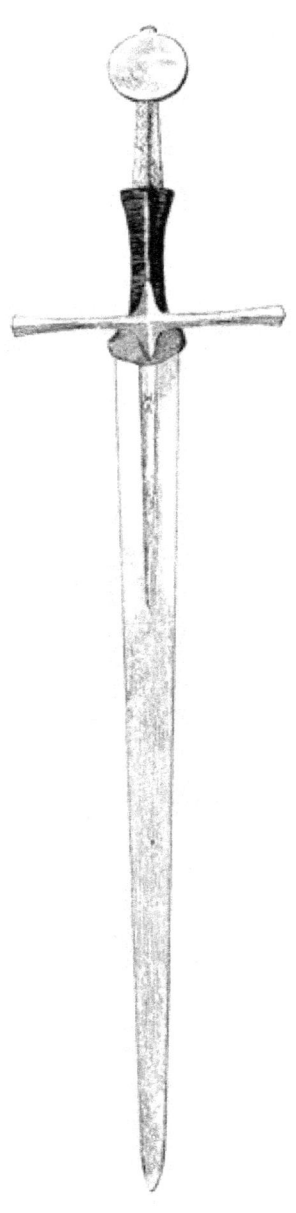

www.ingramcontent.com/pod-product-compliance
Lightning Source LLC
Chambersburg PA
CBHW031942070426
42450CB00005BA/377